SUPER FACTS

BODY

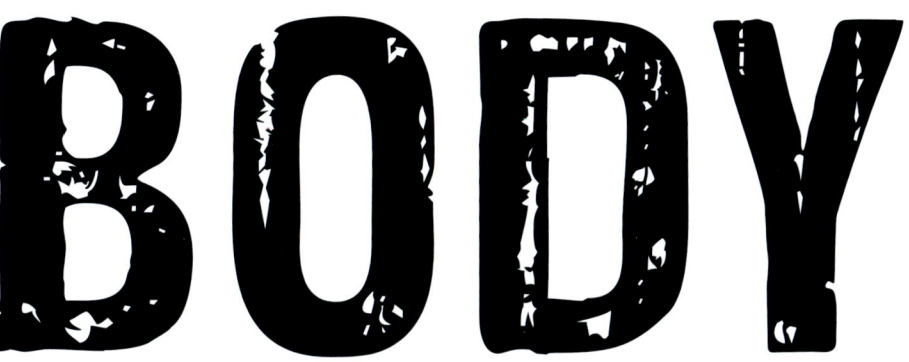

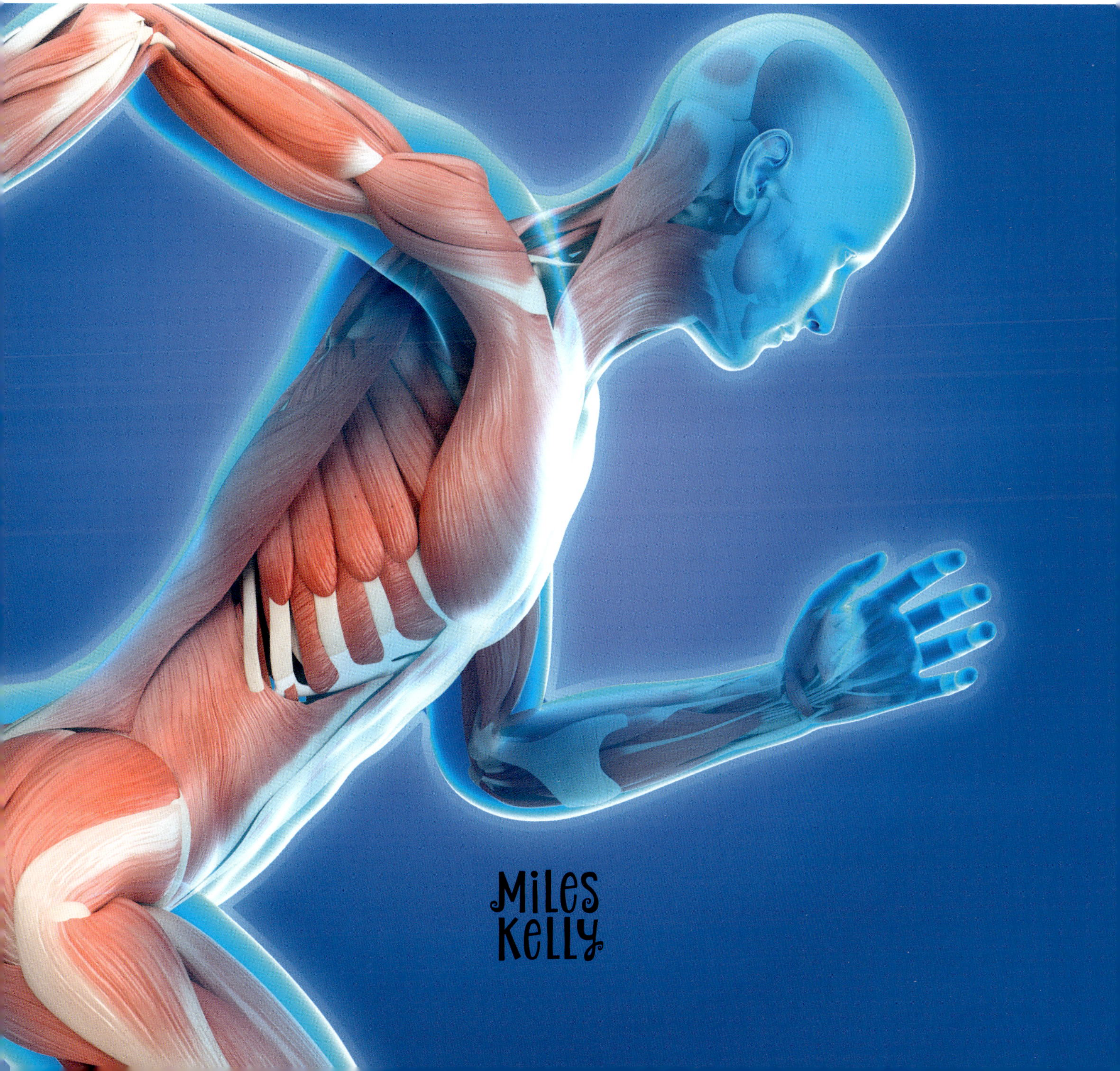

Miles Kelly

Contents

Being human

Body structure

Nervous system

Circulatory system

Digestive and urinary systems

Hormones, development and immunity

The human body

- The human body is made up of millions of cells. These cells make up tissues. Tissues combine to form organs, while organs combine to make the body's main systems.

- Your body systems are interlinked: each has its own task, but they are all dependent on one another.

- The skeleton supports the body, protects major organs, and provides an anchor for the muscles.

- The nervous system is the brain and the nerves – the body's control and communications network.

- The digestive system breaks down food into chemicals that the body can use to its advantage.

- The immune system is the body's defence against germs. It includes white blood cells, antibodies and the lymphatic system.

- Water balance inside the body is controlled by the urinary system. This removes extra water as urine and gets rid of impurities in the blood.

- The respiratory system takes air into the lungs to supply oxygen for the body's cells, while getting rid of unwanted carbon dioxide.

- The reproductive system is the smallest of all the systems. It consists of the sexual organs that enable people to have children. It is the only system that is different in males and females.

- Other body systems include the hormonal system (controls growth and internal coordination by chemical hormones), the integumentary system (skin, hair and nails) and the sensory system (eyes, ears, nose, tongue, skin, balance).

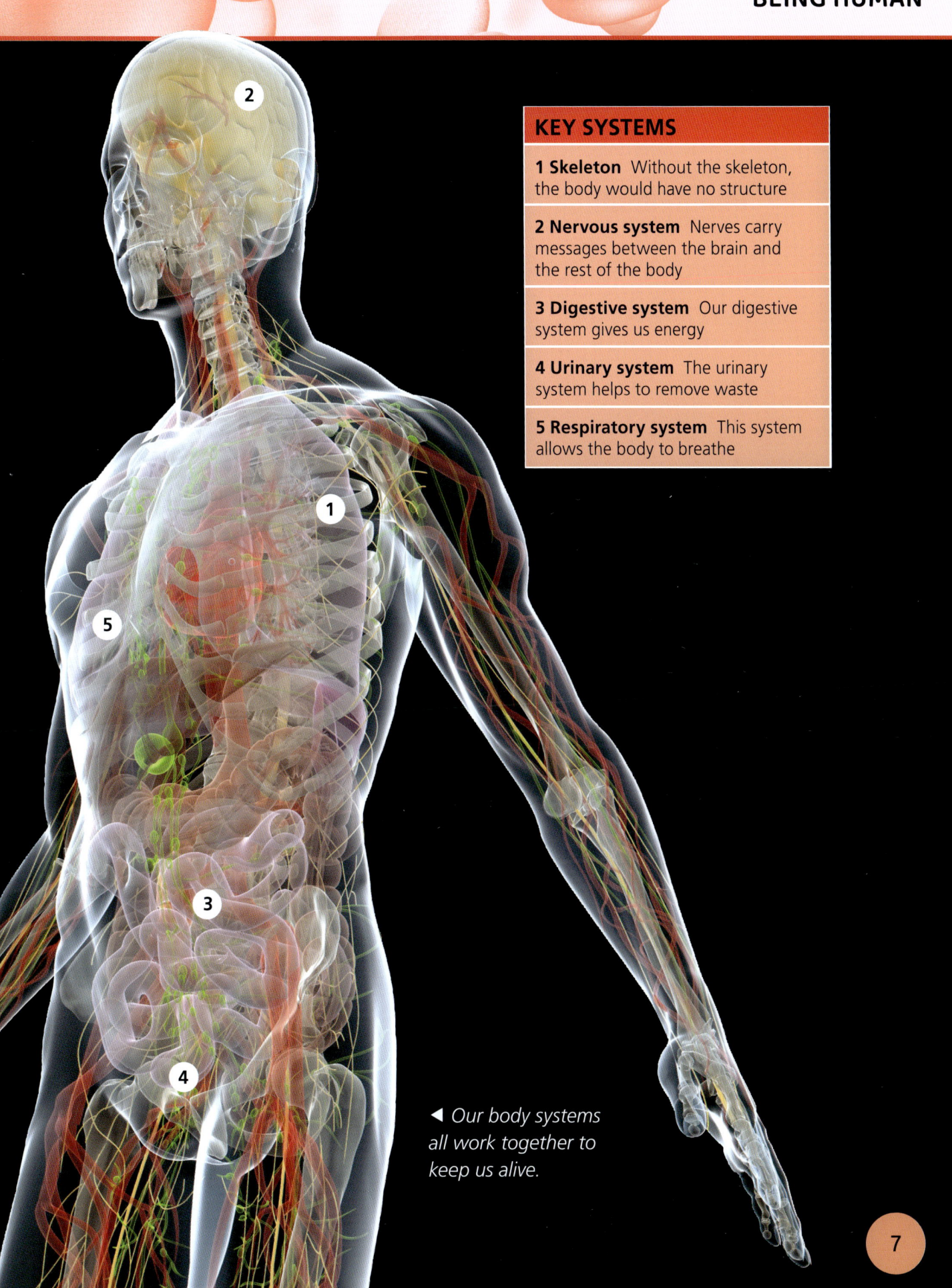

KEY SYSTEMS

1 Skeleton Without the skeleton, the body would have no structure

2 Nervous system Nerves carry messages between the brain and the rest of the body

3 Digestive system Our digestive system gives us energy

4 Urinary system The urinary system helps to remove waste

5 Respiratory system This system allows the body to breathe

◄ *Our body systems all work together to keep us alive.*

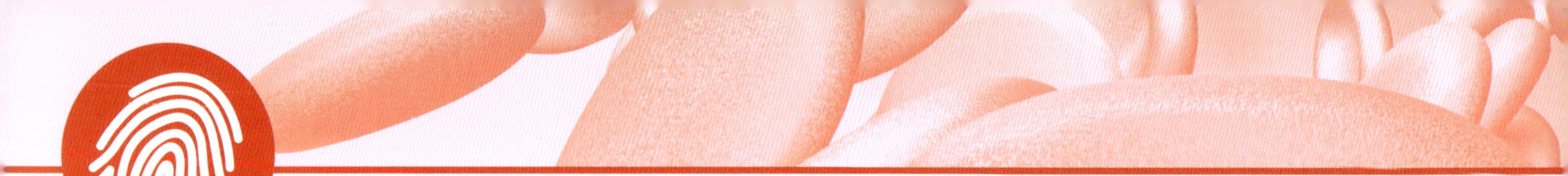

Cells

- Cells are the basic building blocks of your body. Most are so tiny you would need 10,000 of them to cover a pinhead.

- There are over 200 kinds of cell in your body, including nerve cells, skin cells, blood cells, bone cells, fat cells, muscle cells and many more.

- A cell is like a parcel of organic (life) chemicals with a thin membrane (casing) of protein and fat. The membrane holds the cell together, but allows nutrients to get in and waste products to get out.

- Most body cells live for a very short time and are continually being replaced by new ones. The main exceptions are nerve cells – these are long-lasting and are rarely replaced.

- Inside the cell is a liquid called cytoplasm, and floating in this are various minute structures called organelles.

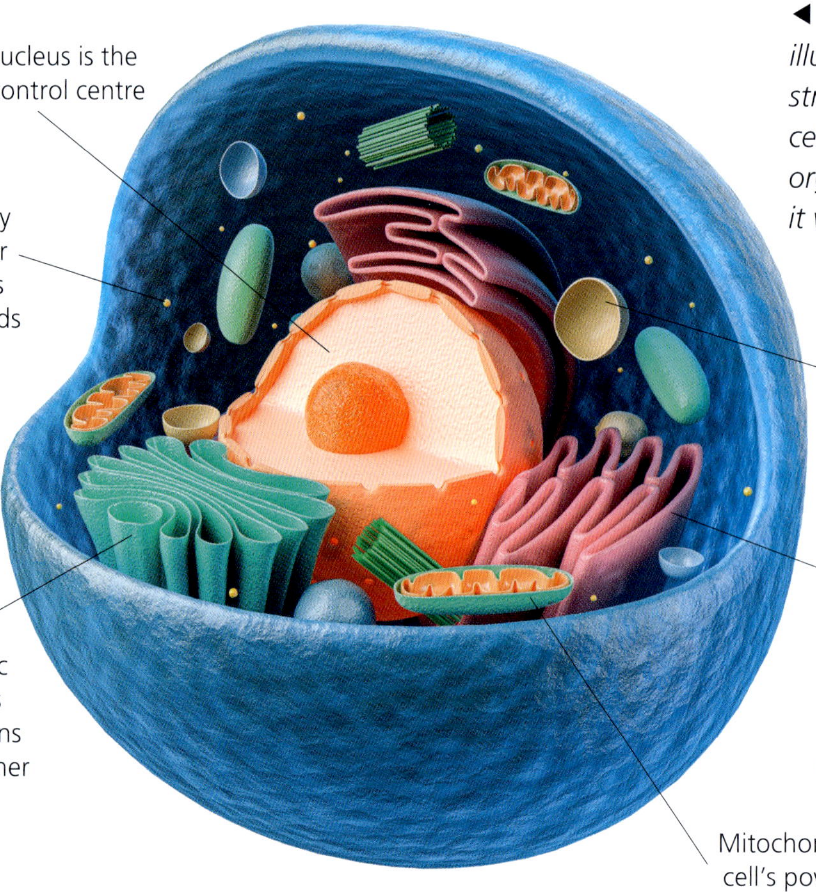

The nucleus is the cell's control centre

Ribosomes form proteins by linking together basic chemicals called amino acids

Endoplasmic reticulum is where proteins are put together

◄ *This cross-section illustration shows the structure of a typical cell, with some of the organelles that keep it working properly.*

Lysosomes are the cell's recycling centres

The Golgi body modifies, sorts and packages proteins, making them ready for their destination

Mitochondria are the cell's power stations

DNA

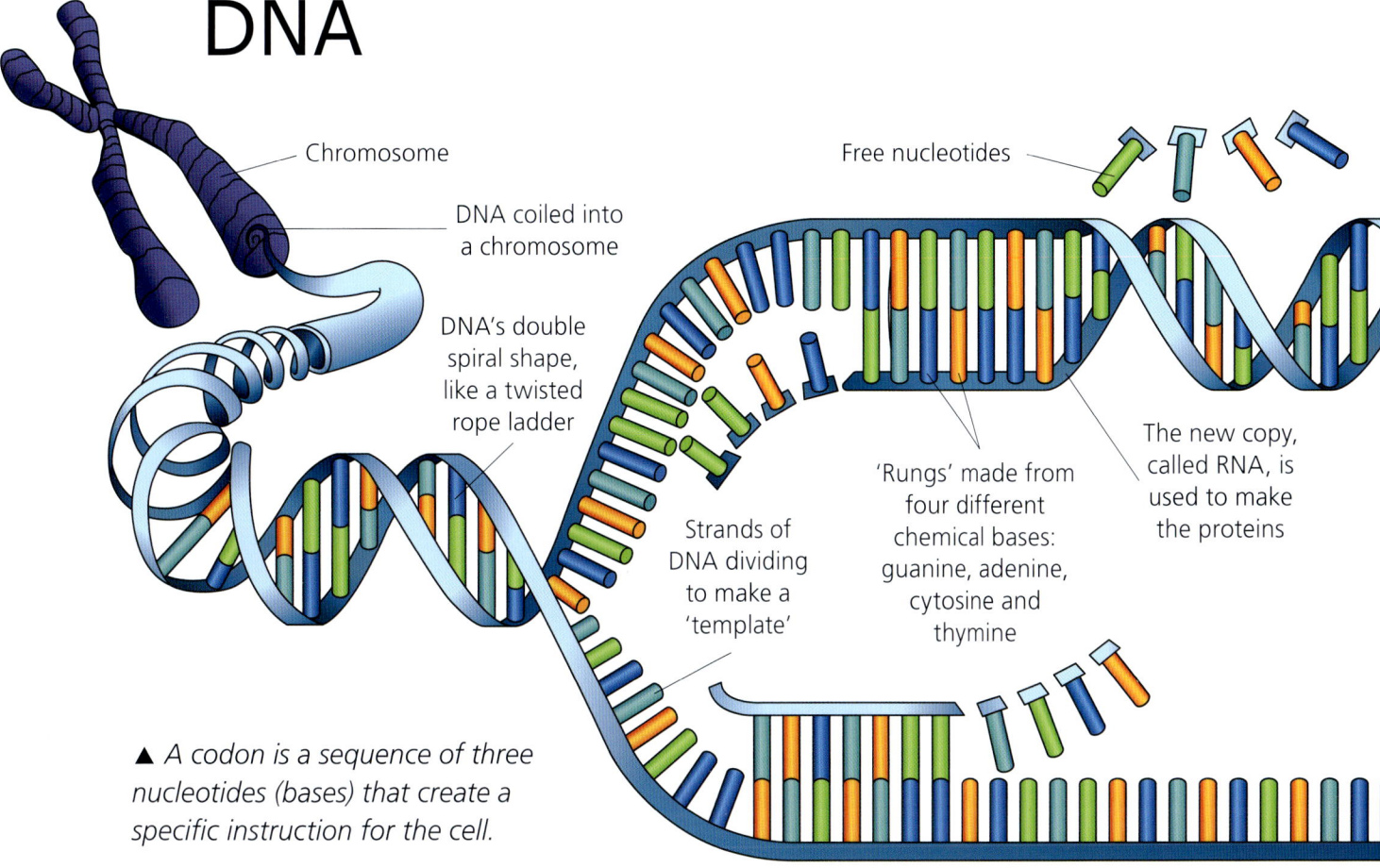

Chromosome

DNA coiled into a chromosome

DNA's double spiral shape, like a twisted rope ladder

Free nucleotides

The new copy, called RNA, is used to make the proteins

'Rungs' made from four different chemical bases: guanine, adenine, cytosine and thymine

Strands of DNA dividing to make a 'template'

▲ *A codon is a sequence of three nucleotides (bases) that create a specific instruction for the cell.*

- DNA (deoxyribonucleic acid) is the molecule inside every cell that carries all your genes, or genetic information. When DNA is needed, it unravels.

- Using evidence revealed by Rosalind Franklin's X-ray image of DNA, its structure was first officially identified in 1953 by James Watson and Francis Crick, who announced they had 'found the secret of life'.

DID YOU KNOW?
If you unravelled all your cells' DNA, it might stretch to more than 100 billion km.

- DNA is shaped in a 'double helix' with linking bars. With the exception of identical twins, no two people have the same DNA sequences.

- Because DNA is responsible for making proteins, it is essential for growth, development and body function.

- When the cell needs to make a new protein, the DNA 'unzips' and the codons are matched by free bases, which make a copy of the DNA.

9

Chromosomes

👋 Chromosomes are the microscopically tiny, twisted threads inside every cell that carry your body's life instructions in chemical form.

👋 You have 23 pairs of chromosomes in each body cell – 46 in total.

👋 One of each chromosome pair came from your mother and the other from your father.

👋 In a girl's 23 chromosome pairs, each half exactly matches the other (the set from the mother is equivalent to the set from the father).

👋 Boys have 22 matching chromosome pairs, but the 23rd pair is made up of two odd, non-matching chromosomes (see below).

A normal body cell
has 46 chromosomes,
divided into 23 pairs

Male

The male sperm
cell has 23
chromosomes

▼ *Two sets of chromosomes,
one each from the mother
and the father, combine
when the egg is fertilized.*

Y chromosome
from the father

At fertilization, the full
set of 46 chromosomes
is restored. In this case,
the result is a boy.

The female
egg cell has 23
chromosomes

X chromosome
from the mother

Female

Genes

- Genes are the body's chemical instructions for your entire life. They hold information relating to growth, survival, to having children and, perhaps, even to dying.

- Individual genes are instructions to make particular proteins – the body's building-block molecules.

- Small sets of genes control features such as the colour of your hair or your eyes, or create a particular body process – such as the digestion of fat from food.

- Each of your body cells (except egg and sperm cells) carries identical sets of genes. This is because all your cells were made by other cells splitting in two, starting with the original egg cell in your mother.

- Your genes are a mixture – half come from your mother and half from your father. However, none of your brothers or sisters will get the same mix, unless you are identical twins.

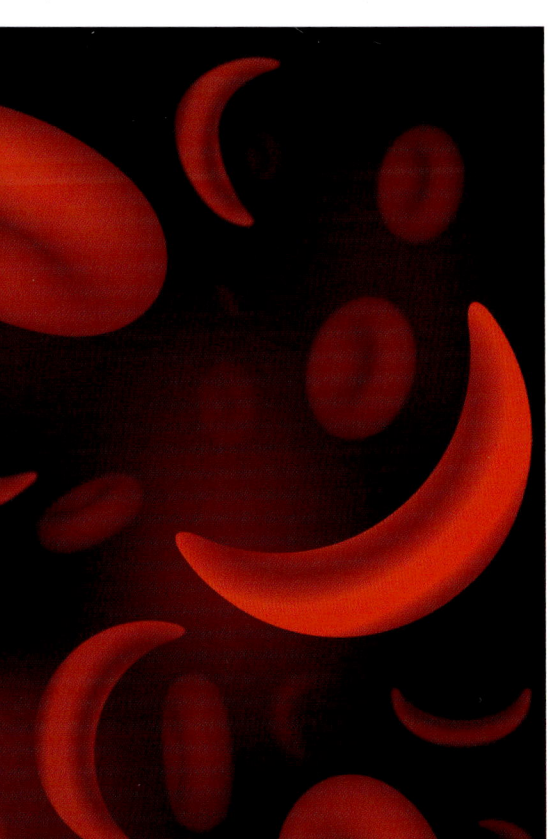

- Genes make us unique – making us tall or short, fair or dark, brilliant dancers or speakers, healthy or likely to suffer from a particular illness, and so on.

- Genes are sections of DNA (see page 9), a microscopically tiny molecule inside each cell.

- Occasionally, genes are faulty. Some faulty or abnormal genes can cause health problems known as genetic disorders.

◀ *Faulty genes can cause illnesses. In sickle cell anaemia, red blood cells (normally round) become crescent-shaped.*

Heredity

- Your 'heredity' is the name we give to all the body characteristics you inherit – genetically – from your parents, whether it is your mother's black hair or your father's knobbly knees, for example!

- Characteristics, or traits, are passed on by the genes carried on your chromosomes (see page 10).

- The basic laws of heredity were discovered by the Austrian monk Gregor Mendel, who studied the traits of plants in the 1850s and '60s.

- Your body characteristics are a mix of two sets of instructions – one from your mother's chromosomes and the other from your father's.

- Each characteristic is the work of only one gene – either your mother's or your father's. This gene is said to be 'expressed'.

- A gene that is not expressed does not vanish. Instead, it stays dormant (asleep) in your chromosomes, and may be passed on to your children.

- When there is no competition from a 'dominant' gene, a 'recessive' gene may be expressed and passed on. This may happen if both of your parents carry the recessive gene.

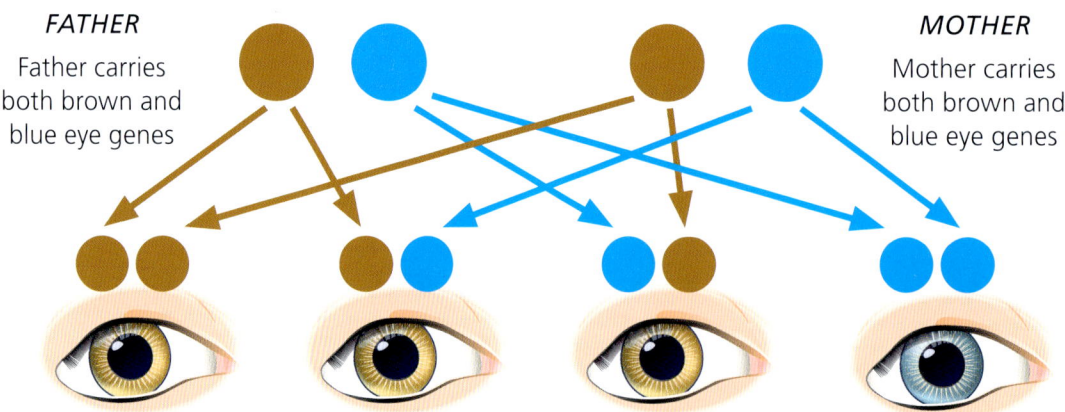

2 brown eye genes = offspring with brown eyes
1 brown eye gene + 1 blue eye gene = offspring with brown eyes
1 blue eye gene + 1 brown eye gene = offspring with brown eyes
2 blue eye genes = offspring with blue eyes

▲ *In this example, both parents have genes for brown and blue eyes. Brown eye genes are dominant, so their offspring are more likely to have brown eyes.*

The human genome

🖐 The human genome consists of all the genes found in the 23 pairs of chromosomes that a normal human being carries.

🖐 Humans have about 20,000–25,000 genes, separated by 'junk' pieces of DNA that have no function. 'Junk' makes up 97 per cent of the human genome.

🖐 Many diseases have a genetic component, or cause. Tests are being developed that look for a tendency to develop certain diseases.

🖐 Scientists may be able to cure some diseases once they know which genes cause them, and where on the genome they are located.

🖐 Approximately 99.9 per cent of all human genes are identical. It is the 0.1 per cent variation that makes us all completely unique.

🖐 Scientists can use this 0.1 per cent difference to compare samples of DNA and identify people who leave traces of DNA at a crime scene.

▼ *Normally, humans have two copies of every chromosome. Down's syndrome is caused by the presence of three copies of chromosome 21, as shown below.*

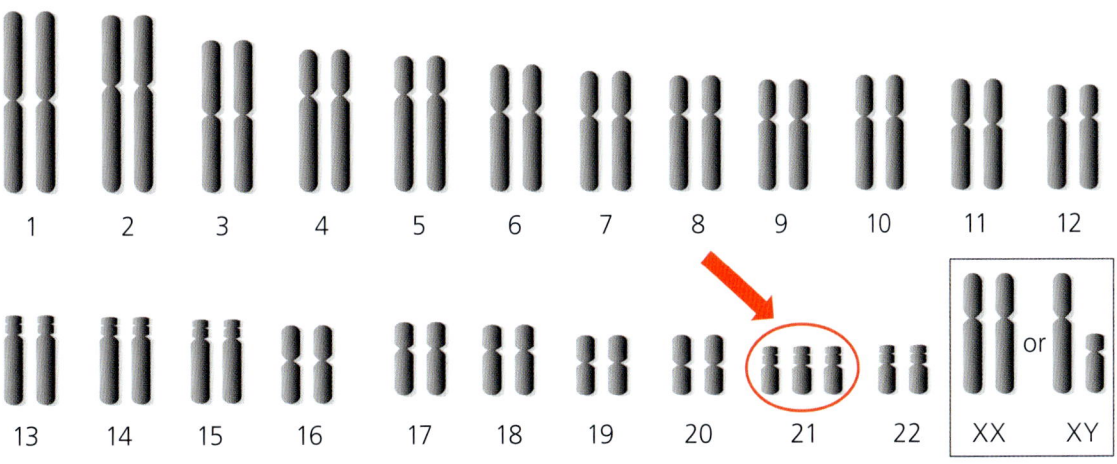

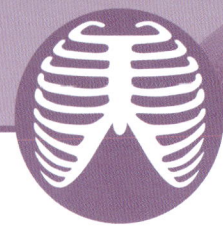

Tissues

- A tissue is a body substance made from many of the same type of cell. Muscle cells make muscle tissue, nerve cells form nerve tissue, and so on.

- Connective tissue holds all the other kinds of tissue together in various ways. The adipose tissue, which makes fat, tendons and cartilage, is connective tissue.

- Bone and blood are both connective tissues.

- Skin is made from epithelial tissue. This tissue may combine three kinds of cell to make a thin, waterproof layer – squamous (flat), cuboid (box-like) and columnar (pillar-like) cells.

- Nerve tissue is made mostly from neurons (nerve cells), plus the Schwann cells that coat them.

- The heart is made mostly of muscle tissue, but also includes epithelial and connective tissue.

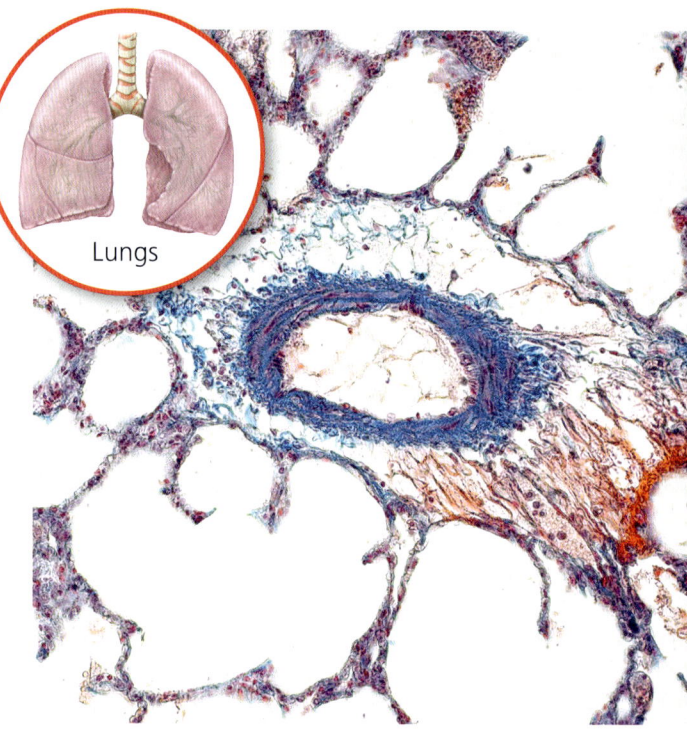

Lungs

▲ Lungs are largely made from special lung tissues, but the mucous membrane that lines the airways is epithelial tissue.

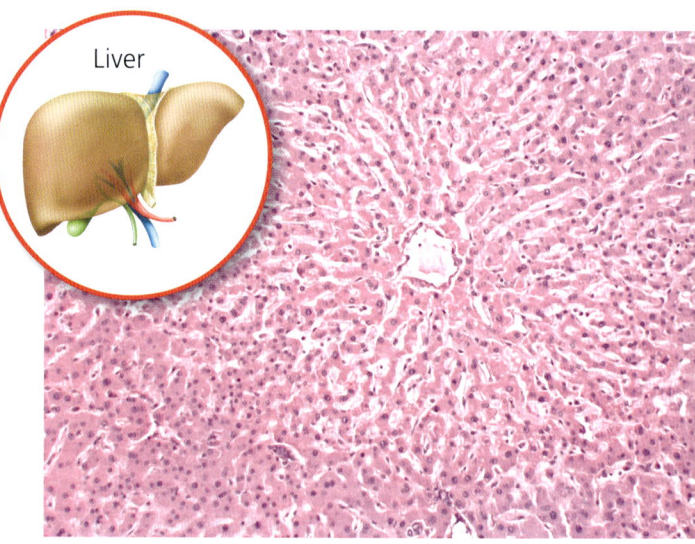

Liver

▲ Liver tissue is made from densely packed liver cells, as shown in this highly magnified photograph.

DID YOU KNOW?
Your body is entirely made up of tissues and fluid.

Organs

- A collection of related organs form a body system.

- Body organs work together to keep the body functioning.

- The largest organ is the skin, which covers the whole body.

- The smallest organ is the pineal gland, a tiny organ in the brain that produces a substance that affects sleep.

- We can survive without some organs.

ORGAN	WHAT IT DOES
BRAIN	Controls the nervous system and many organs
HEART	Keeps blood flowing around the body
LUNGS	Enable us to get oxygen from the air as we respire (breathe)
VOICE BOX	Produces sounds that we turn into speech
STOMACH	Involved in the storage, churning and breakdown of food
LIVER	Produces chemicals essential for survival
GALLBLADDER	Assists with the digestion of food
PANCREAS	Helps to control sugar levels in the body
SPLEEN	Produces cells that help to fight infections
SMALL INTESTINE	Processes food and absorbs useful substances
APPENDIX	Has no known use in humans
LARGE INTESTINE	Absorbs water from food and gets rid of waste
KIDNEYS	Help to control the body's fluid balance
BLADDER	Stores urine
SKIN	A protective covering over the body

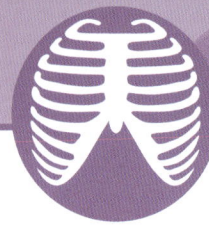

Skin

- Skin is your protective coat, shielding your body from the weather and from infection, and helping to keep it at just the right temperature.

- It is also your largest sense receptor, responding to touch, pressure, heat and cold.

- Skin uses sunlight to makes vitamin D for your body.

- The epidermis (the skin's thin, outer layer) is just dead cells.

- This top layer, the epidermis, is mainly made up of a tough protein called keratin – the remains of skin cells that die off.

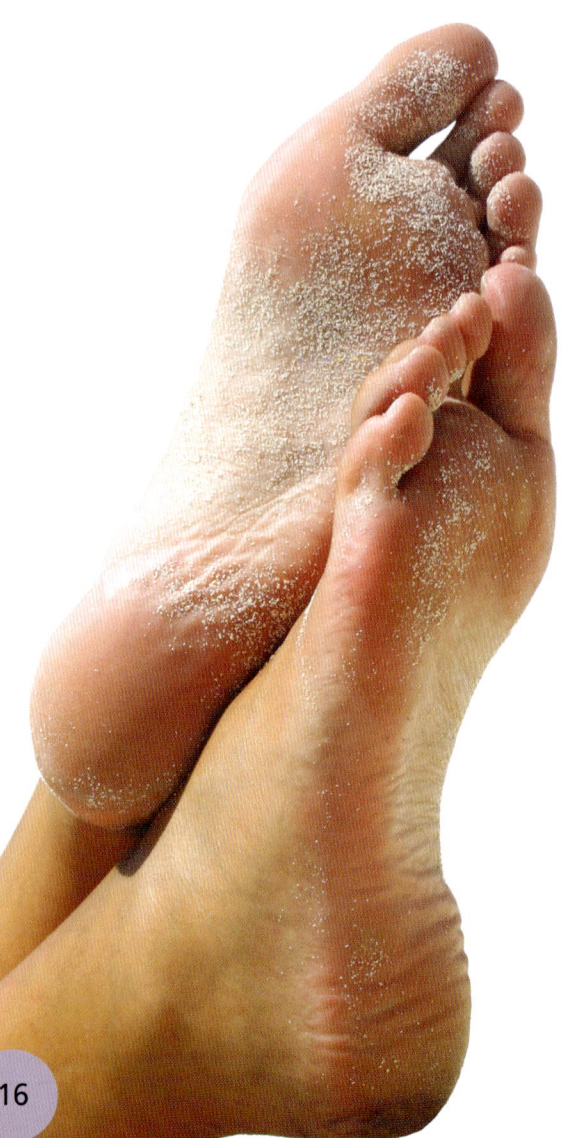

- Below the epidermis is a thick layer of living cells called the dermis, which contains the sweat glands.

- Skin is 6 mm thick on the soles of your feet, while the skin on your eyelids is just 0.5 mm thick.

- Your body sheds around 50,000 flakes of skin in a minute.

- Sweat glands help to regulate (control) your body temperature by releasing sweat to cool the skin's surface.

◄ *The skin on the sole of your foot is hairless and thicker than anywhere else on your body.*

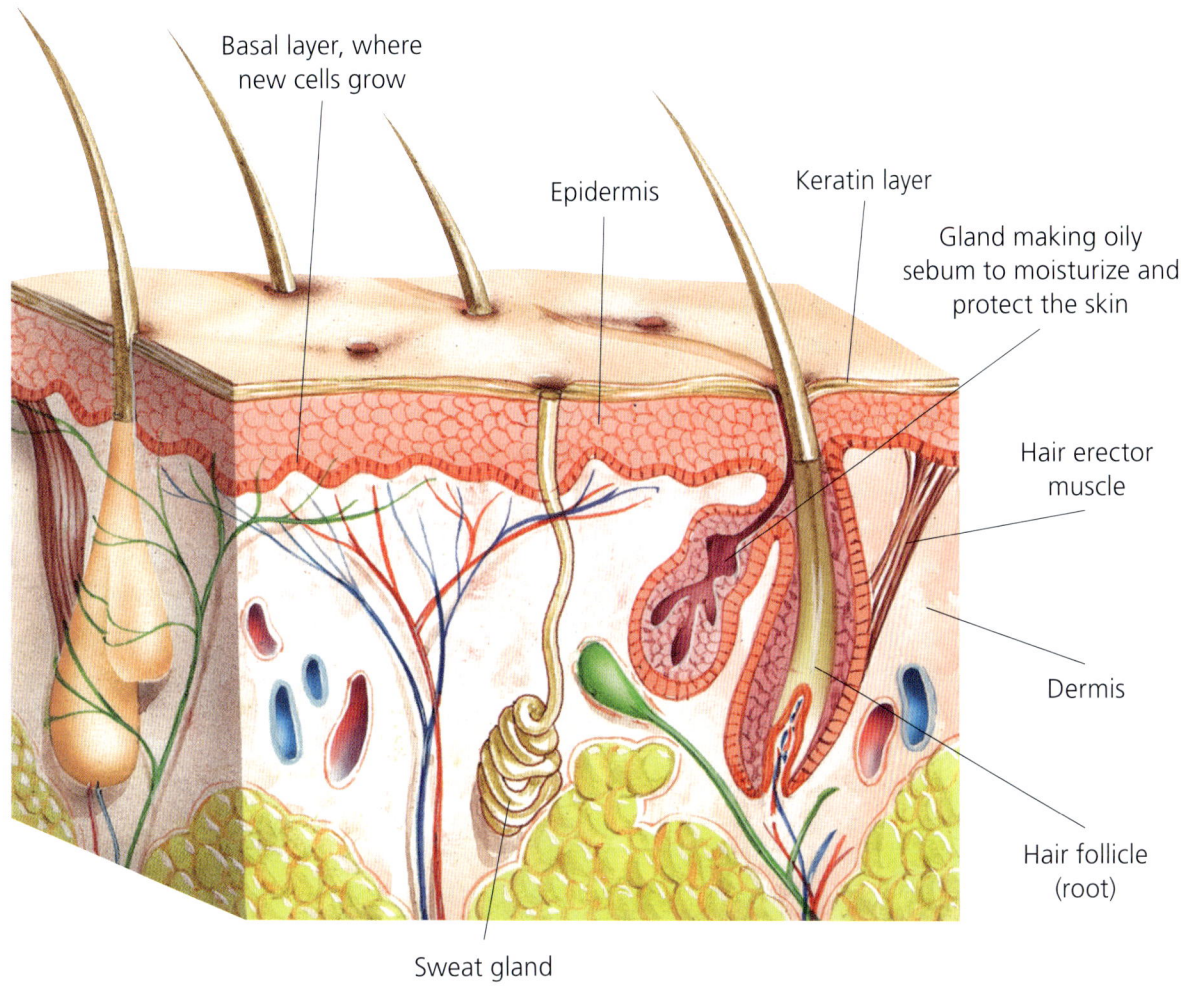

Basal layer, where new cells grow

Epidermis

Keratin layer

Gland making oily sebum to moisturize and protect the skin

Hair erector muscle

Dermis

Hair follicle (root)

Sweat gland

▶ *This is a cross-section of skin, hugely magnified, showing its key components (parts).*

- Hair roots have tiny muscles that pull the hair upright when you are cold, giving you 'goose bumps'.

- The epidermis contains cells that make the dark pigment melanin. This gives dark-skinned people their colour and fair-skinned people a tan.

DID YOU KNOW?
Even though its thickness averages just 2 mm, your skin gets an eighth of all your blood supply.

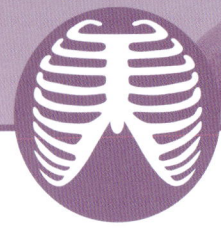

Hair

- Humans are one of very few land mammals to have almost bare skin. But they still do have some hair.

- Lanugo is the very fine hair that babies are covered in when they are inside the womb, from the fourth month of pregnancy onwards.

- Vellus hair is the fine hair that grows all over your body until you reach puberty.

- Terminal hair is the coarser hair on your head, as well as the hair that grows on a man's chin and around an adult's genitals.

- The colour of your hair depends on the amount you have of pigments called melanin and carotene in the hairs.

- Hair is red or auburn if it contains carotene. Black, brown and blonde hairs get their colour from black melanin.

- Each hair is rooted in a pit called the hair follicle.

- Hairs grow as cells fill with a material called keratin – and then die off, piling up inside the follicles.

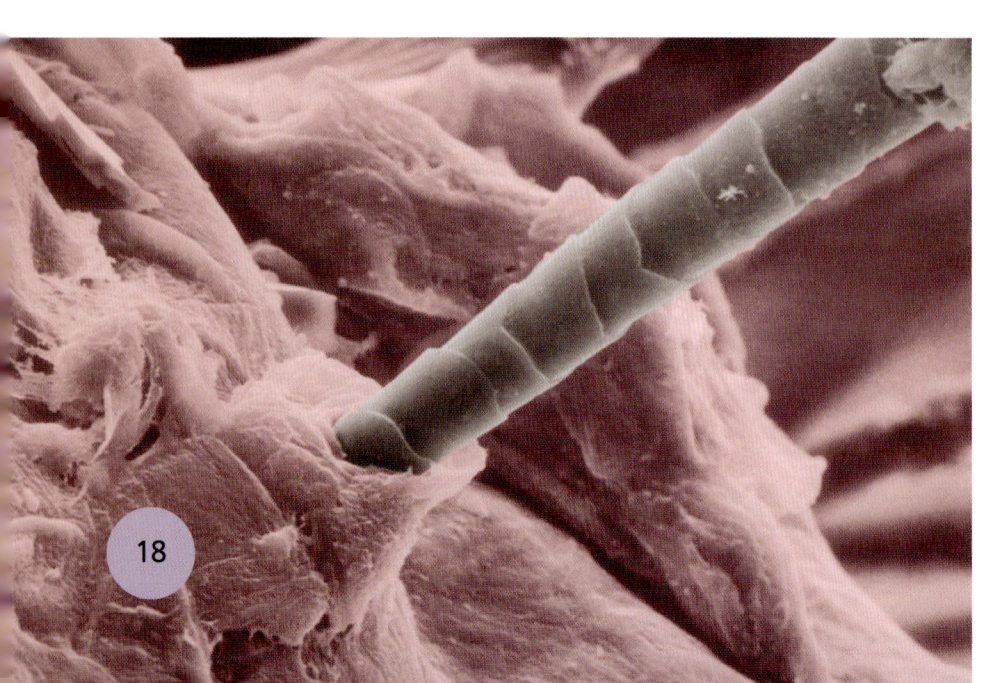

◄ A microscopic view of a hair. It is alive and growing in the base of the follicle. The hair that sticks out of the skin is dead, and is made up of flat cells stuck together.

18

Nails

Nails protect the ends of our fingers and toes. They are formed of dead cells – and strengthened by a protein called keratin.

Without nails, we would not be able to scratch. They also help us to judge pressure when picking up objects.

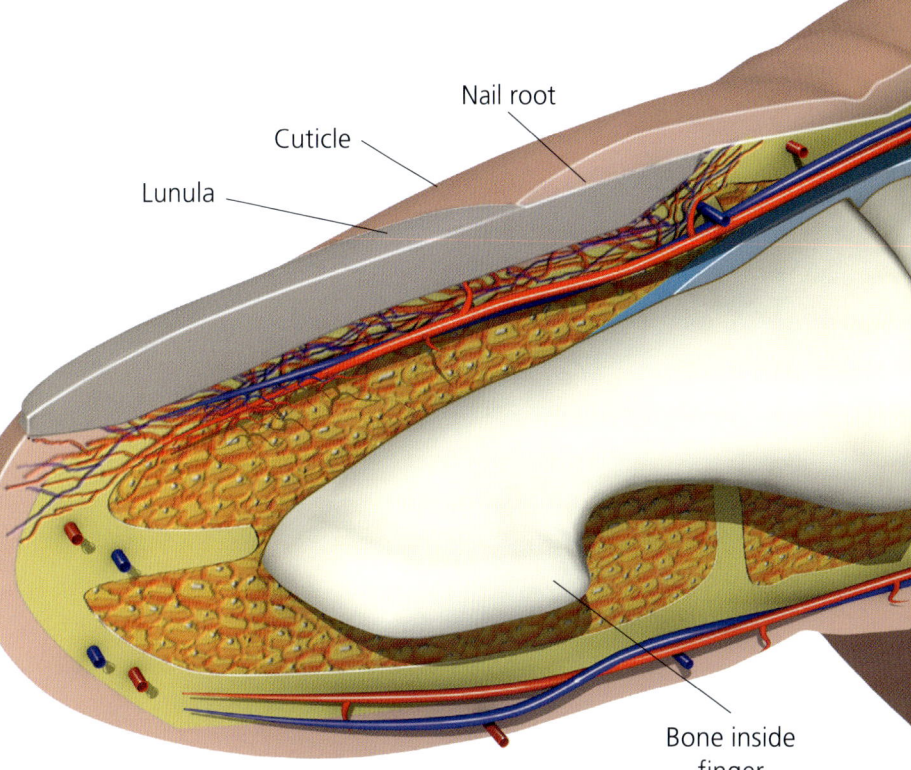

Cuticle

Lunula

Nail root

Bone inside finger

▲ A nail has its root under the skin and grows along the nail bed – the skin underneath it.

Nails grow from a nail root, which is hidden by a fold of skin at the base of the nail called a cuticle.

The pale 'half moon' at the base of the nail is called the lunula, after the Latin word for the 'moon'.

Most nails only grow by about 0.5 mm each month. Fingernails grow faster than toenails do.

Nails grow faster in summer than in winter.

The nails on your right hand will grow more quickly than the nails on your left hand, if you are right-handed. If you are left-handed, the nails on your left hand will grow faster.

DID YOU KNOW?
It can take up to six months for a lost fingernail and 18 months for a lost toenail to regrow completely.

19

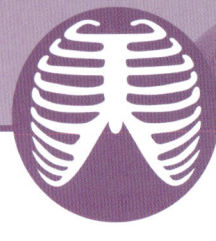

Teeth and gums

- Milk teeth are the 20 teeth that start to appear at six months old.

- At around six years old, 32 adult teeth start to appear – 16 at the top and 16 at the bottom.

- Molars are the big, strong teeth at the back of the mouth. There are usually six pairs. Their flattish tops are shaped for grinding food.

- The four molars at the back of the jaw are the wisdom teeth. These are the last to grow – and sometimes they never appear at all.

- Premolars are the four pairs of teeth in front of the molars.

- Incisors are the four pairs of teeth at the front of your mouth. They have sharp edges for cutting food.

- Canines are the two pairs of big, pointed teeth behind the incisors. Their shape is good for tearing up food.

- The enamel on teeth is the body's hardest substance.

▶ *Teeth have roots that slot into the jawbones, but they sit in a fleshy ridge called the gums.*

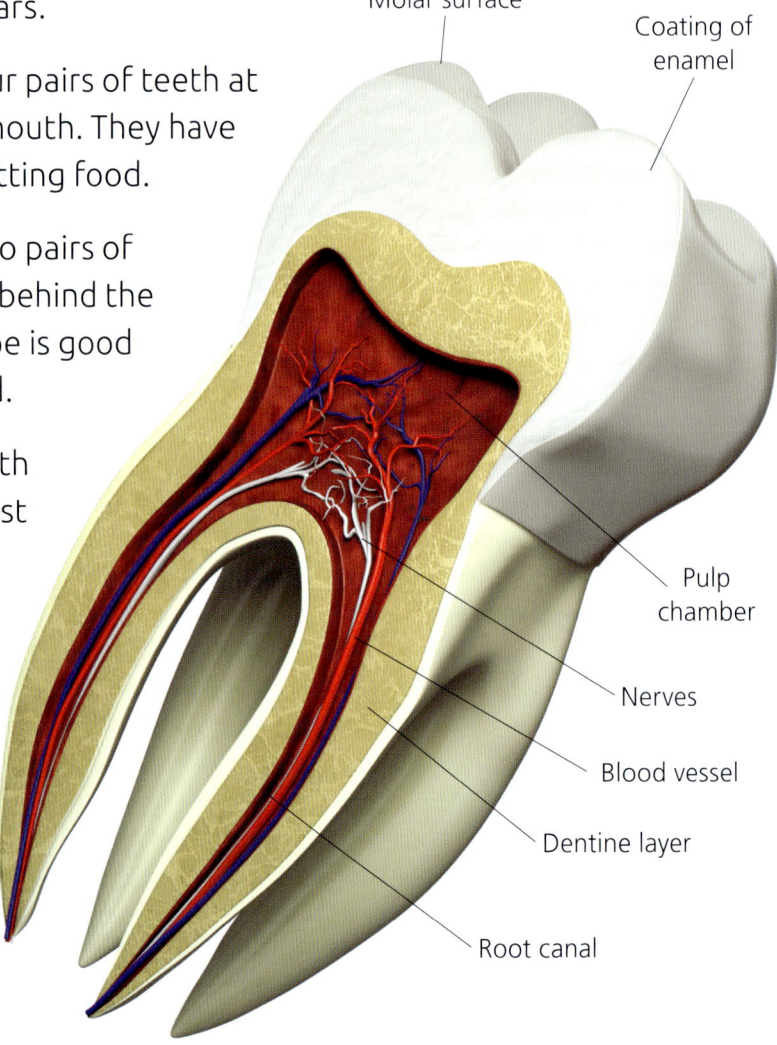

Molar surface

Coating of enamel

Pulp chamber

Nerves

Blood vessel

Dentine layer

Root canal

Bones

- Weight for weight, bone is at least five times as strong as steel.

- Bones are so light they only make up about 3 to 15 per cent of the body's total weight.

- Bones are rigid because of hard deposits of minerals such as calcium and phosphate.

- Bones get their flexibility from tough, elastic fibres of collagen.

- The hard, outer layer of bones (known as compact bone) is reinforced by strong rods called osteons.

- Spongy bone is mainly found on the inside of long bones. It has a light 'honeycomb' structure of thin struts, or tabuculae, angled to absorb stress.

- The core of some bones, such as the long bones in an arm or leg, contains the soft, fatty tissue known as bone marrow.

▶ *Bones are strong but very light because, on the inside, there are many hollow spaces.*

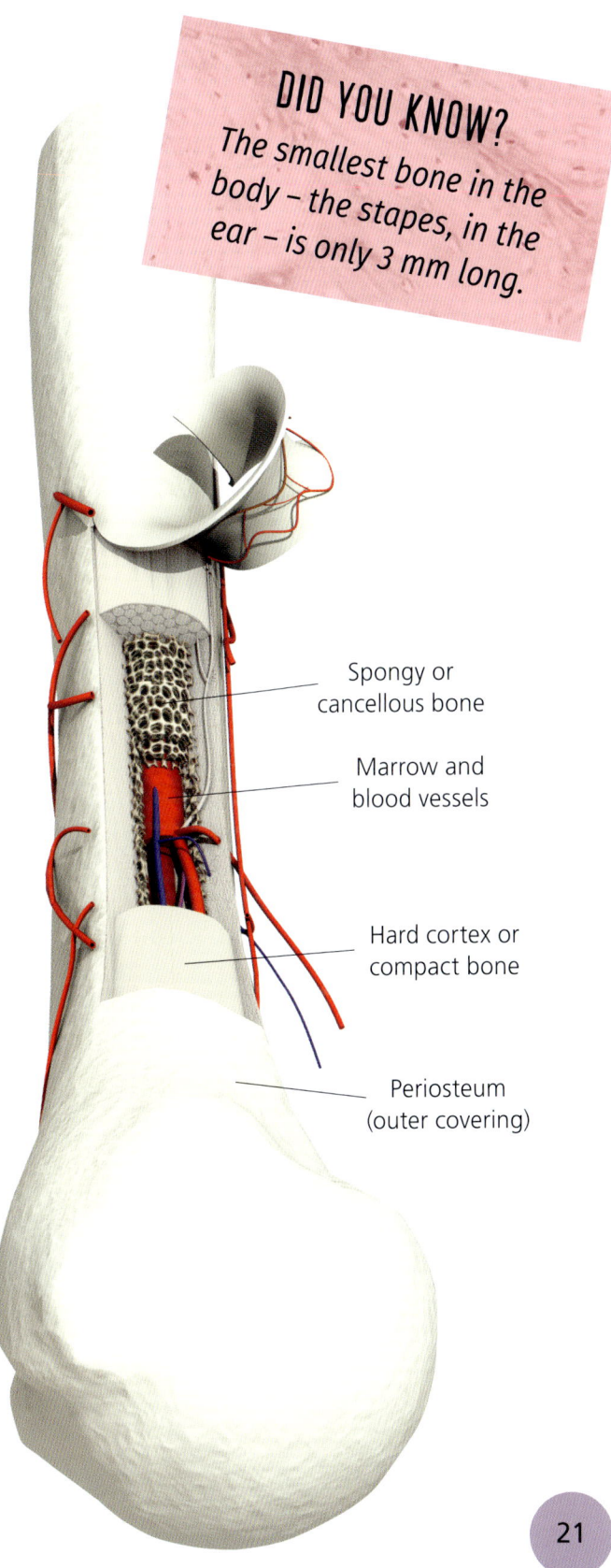

DID YOU KNOW?
The smallest bone in the body – the stapes, in the ear – is only 3 mm long.

Spongy or cancellous bone

Marrow and blood vessels

Hard cortex or compact bone

Periosteum (outer covering)

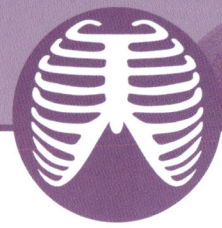

The skeleton

- Your skeleton is a rigid framework of bones, which provides an anchor for your muscles, protects the internal organs and supports your skin and other organs.

- An adult's skeleton has 206 bones, joined together by rubbery cartilage. Some people have extra vertebrae (the bones that make up the backbone, or spine).

- A baby's skeleton has 300 or more bones, but some of these fuse (join) together as the baby grows.

- The parts of an adult skeleton that have fused into one bone (since the infant stage) include the skull and the pelvis.

- The skeleton has two main parts – the axial bones and the appendicular bones.

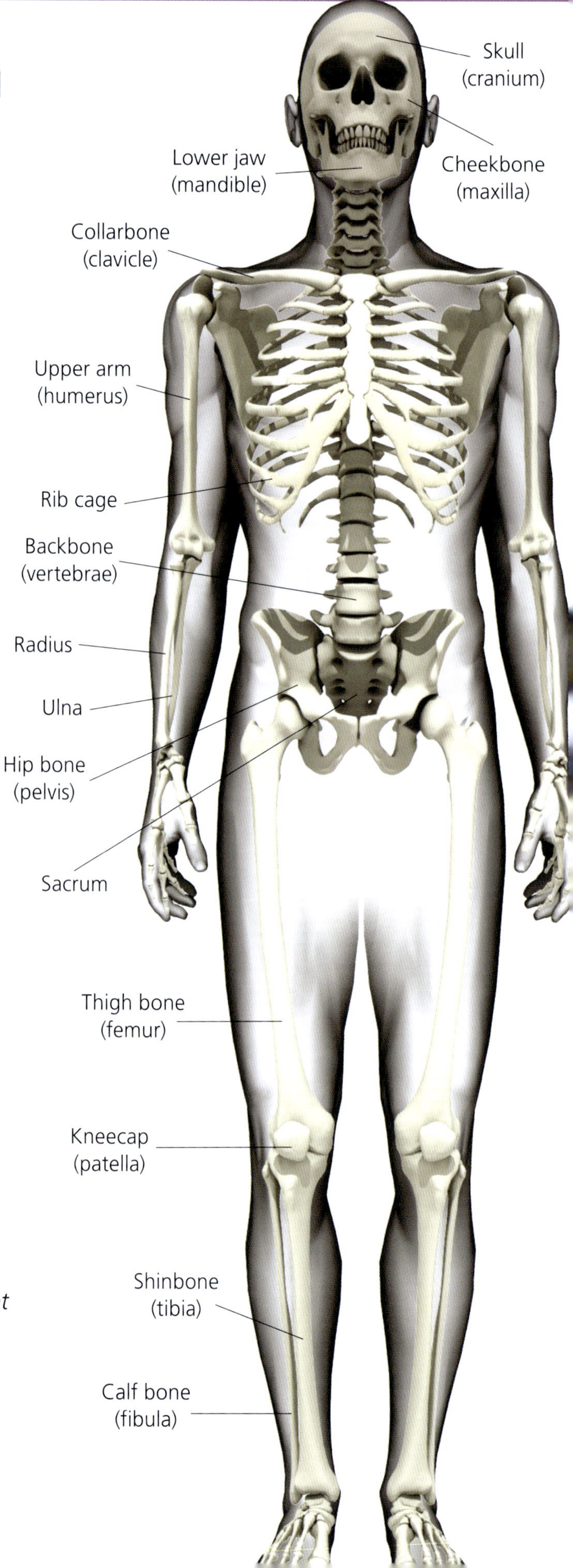

▶ *Your skeleton is the remarkably light, but very tough framework of bones that supports your body. It is made up of more than 200 bones.*

Skull (cranium)

Lower jaw (mandible)

Cheekbone (maxilla)

Collarbone (clavicle)

Upper arm (humerus)

Rib cage

Backbone (vertebrae)

Radius

Ulna

Hip bone (pelvis)

Sacrum

Thigh bone (femur)

Kneecap (patella)

Shinbone (tibia)

Calf bone (fibula)

The axial skeleton consists of the 80 bones of the upper body. It includes the skull, the vertebrae of the backbone, the ribs and the breastbone. The arm and shoulder bones are suspended from it.

The appendicular skeleton is made up of the other 126 bones – the arm and shoulder bones, and the leg and hip bones.

Most women and girls have smaller and lighter skeletons than men and boys.

DID YOU KNOW?
The word 'skeleton' comes from the ancient Greek word for 'dry'.

▼ *Muscles pull and push against the bones of the skeleton to enable us to move, run and walk.*

23

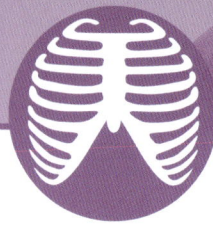

The skull

- The skull or cranium is the hard bone case that contains and protects the brain.

- Although it looks as though the skull is a single bone, it is actually made up of 22 separate bones, fused together.

- The dome on top is called the cranial vault, which is made from eight curved pieces of bone fused (joined) together.

- The skull has four large cavities (spaces) – the cranial cavity for the brain, the nasal cavity (the nose) and two 'orbits' for the eyes.

- There are holes in the skull to allow blood vessels and nerves through, including the optic nerves to the eyes and the olfactory tracts to the nose.

- The biggest hole is in the base of the skull: the brain stem goes through this gap to connect with the spinal cord.

▶ *The skull holds and protects the brain. It is made up of a number of bones that are fused together.*

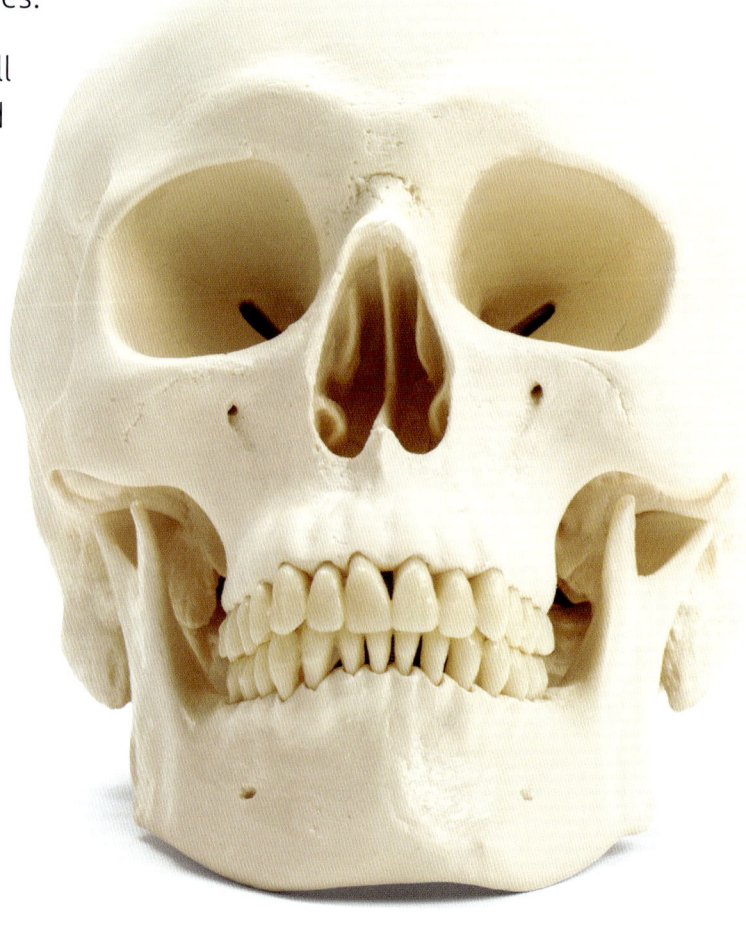

The backbone

- The backbone, otherwise known as the spine, extends from the base of the skull down to the hips.

- It is not a single bone, but a column of drum-shaped bones known as vertebrae (singular: vertebra).

- There are 33 vertebrae in total, although some of these fuse or join together as the body grows.

- Each vertebra is linked to the next by small 'facet' joints, which provide limited movement.

- The vertebrae are separated by discs of rubbery material called cartilage. These cushion the bones and absorb shock when you run and jump.

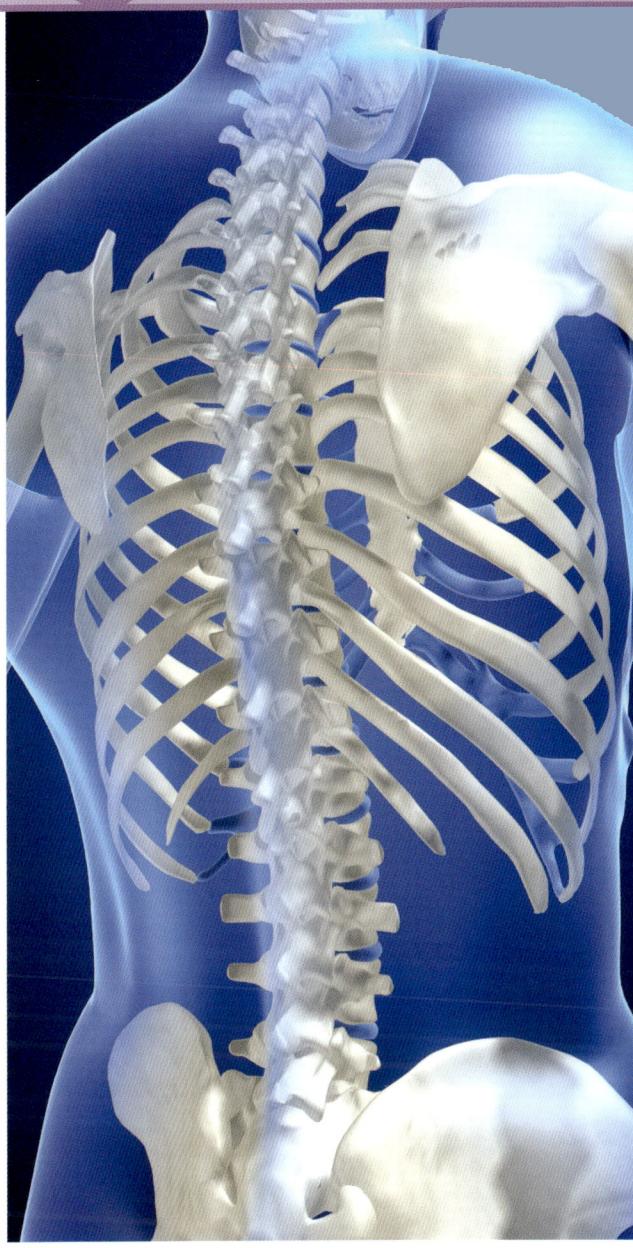

▲ The backbone is not straight – its 33 vertebrae curve into an S-shape.

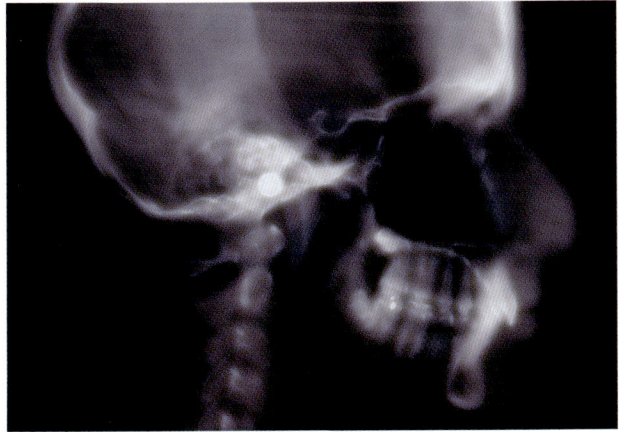

▲ The joint between the top two bones of the spine allows you to turn your head.

DID YOU KNOW?
Gravity squashes the joints in the spine, so you are shorter in the evening than you are in the morning.

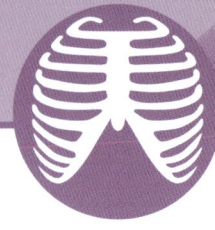

Ribs

The ribs are the thin, flattish bones that curve around your chest.

Together, the rib bones make up the rib cage, with 12 pairs altogether.

The rib cage protects the backbone and breastbone, as well as your vital organs, such as the heart, lungs, liver, kidneys, stomach and spleen.

Gaps between the ribs, called intercostal spaces, contain thin sheets of muscle that expand and relax the chest during breathing.

▼ *The ribs provide a framework for the chest and form a protective cage around the heart, lungs and other organs.*

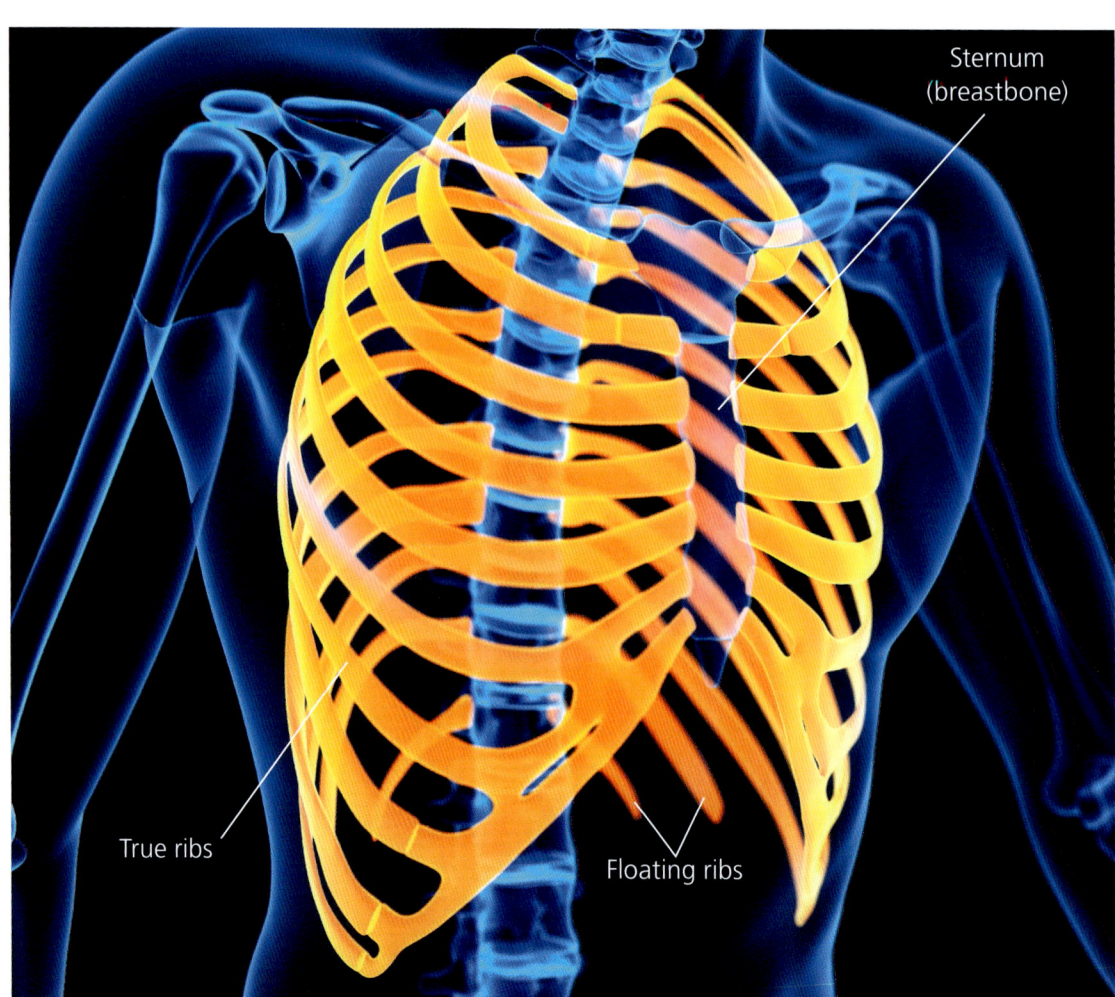

Sternum (breastbone)

True ribs

Floating ribs

The pelvis

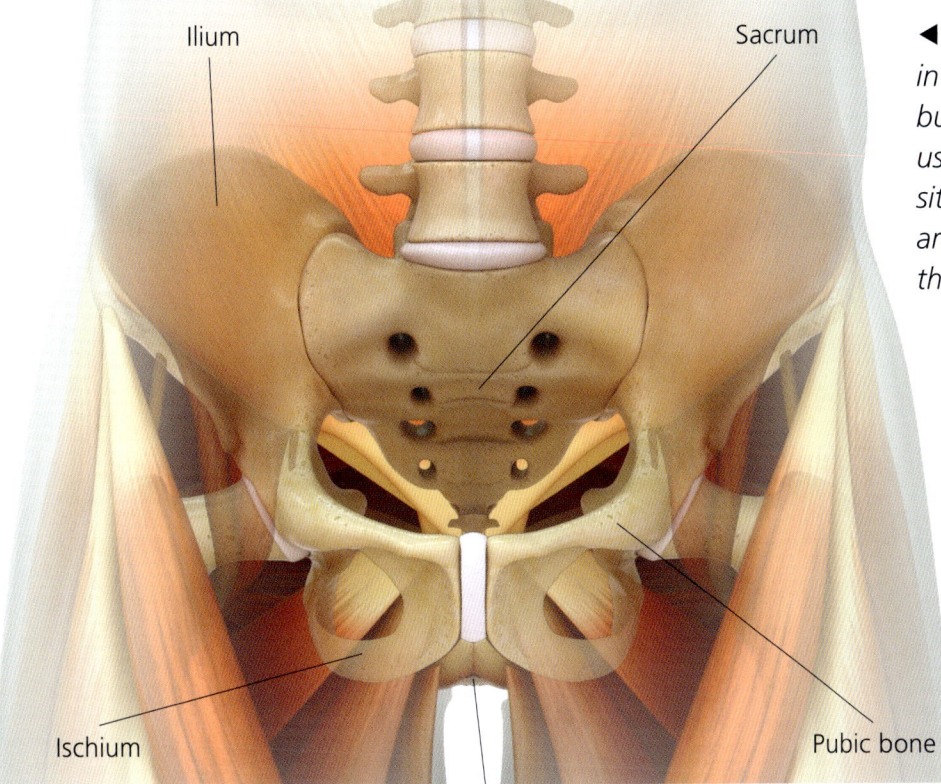

Ilium

Sacrum

◄ *Strong muscles in the thigh and buttocks enable us to walk and sit. These muscles are attached to the pelvis.*

◄ *The two main halves of the pelvis connect to the sacrum, a triangular bone at the base of the spine.*

Ischium

Pubic bone

Pubic symphysis connects the left and right pubic bones

- The pelvis is made up of two hips, consisting of three bones (the ilium, pubis and ischium) which fuse together at puberty.

- Organs in the lower part of the abdomen, such as the bladder and the female reproductive organs, are protected by the pelvis.

- The pelvis also supports the weight of the upper body and helps to transfer weight to and from the legs during standing and walking.

- The human pelvis is shaped to allow us to walk upright easily.

- In women and girls, the pelvis is much wider than in men and boys. This is to allow females to give birth (have babies).

- Forensic scientists can study the differences in pelvis shape to tell whether a skeleton belonged to a male or a female.

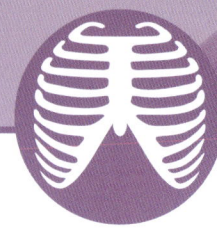

Joints

- Body joints are places where bones meet. There are approximately 400 joints in the human body.

- Every time you sit, stand or move in any way, you are using your joints.

- Joints provide flexibility by allowing movement and create stability by holding bones together.

- Most body joints allow bones to move, but some types of joint only let them move in certain ways.

- Only fixed joints, such as those in the skull, allow zero movement.

- All other joints contain cartilage to cushion the ends of the bones. Some joints also contain fluid to reduce friction between the bones.

- Synovial joints are flexible joints, lubricated with oily 'synovial fluid' and cushioned by cartilage.

DID YOU KNOW?
You have around 27 small joints in each hand and wrist.

◄ *Gymnasts must have supple, flexible joints in order to perform complicated positions and routines.*

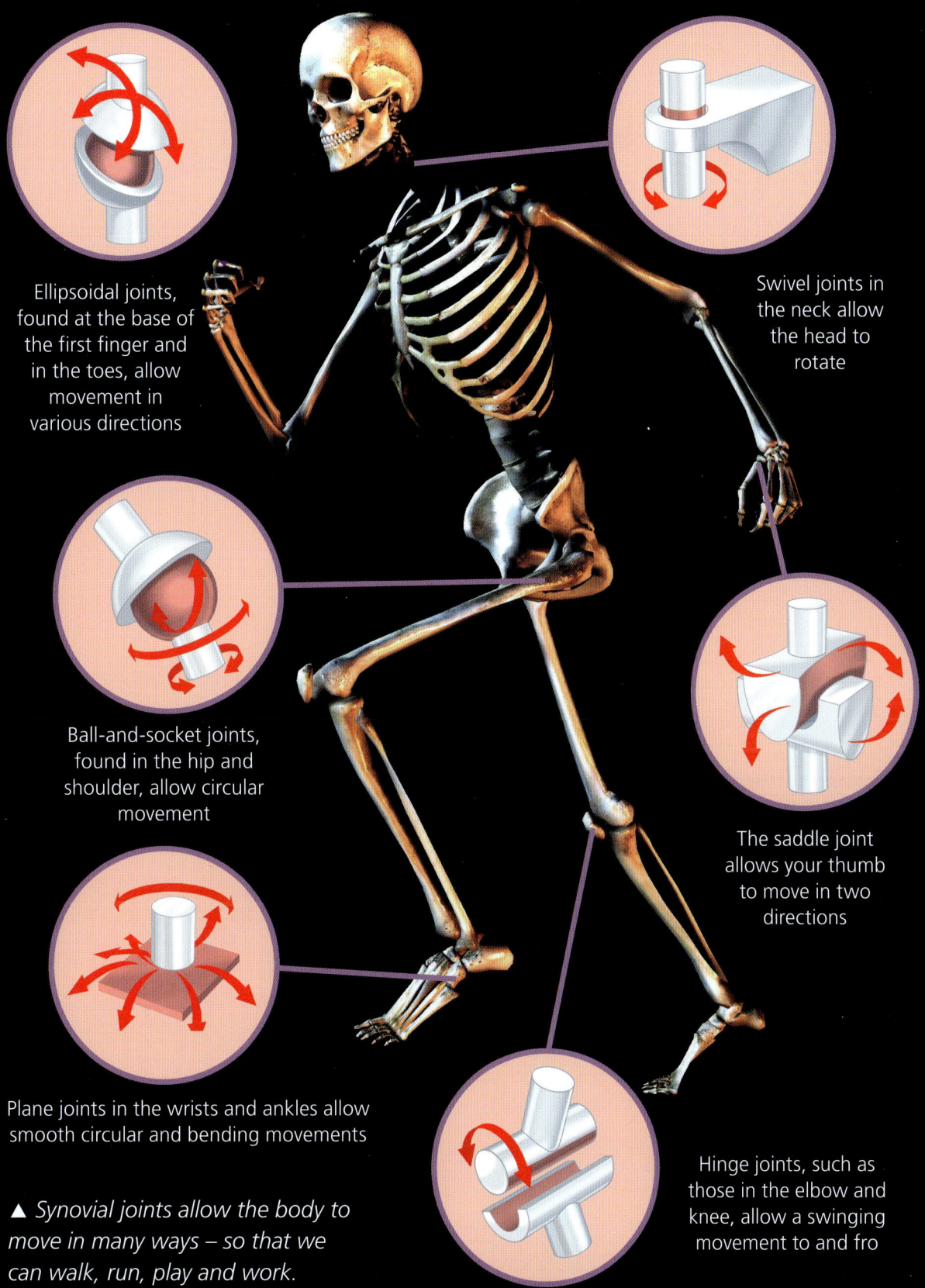

Ellipsoidal joints, found at the base of the first finger and in the toes, allow movement in various directions

Swivel joints in the neck allow the head to rotate

Ball-and-socket joints, found in the hip and shoulder, allow circular movement

The saddle joint allows your thumb to move in two directions

Plane joints in the wrists and ankles allow smooth circular and bending movements

▲ *Synovial joints allow the body to move in many ways – so that we can walk, run, play and work.*

Hinge joints, such as those in the elbow and knee, allow a swinging movement to and fro

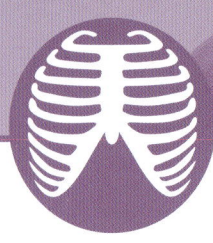

Cartilage

- Cartilage is a rubbery substance found in the body. You can feel the cartilage in your ear if you move it backwards and forwards.

- Cartilage is made from chondrocytes – cells embedded in a jellylike substance with fibres of collagen, all wrapped in tough fibres.

- There are three types of cartilage: hyaline, fibrous and elastic.

- Hyaline cartilage is the most widespread in your body. It's between many of the joints and bones to cushion them against impacts.

- Fibrous cartilage is a really tough form of cartilage used in between the bones of the spine and in the knee.

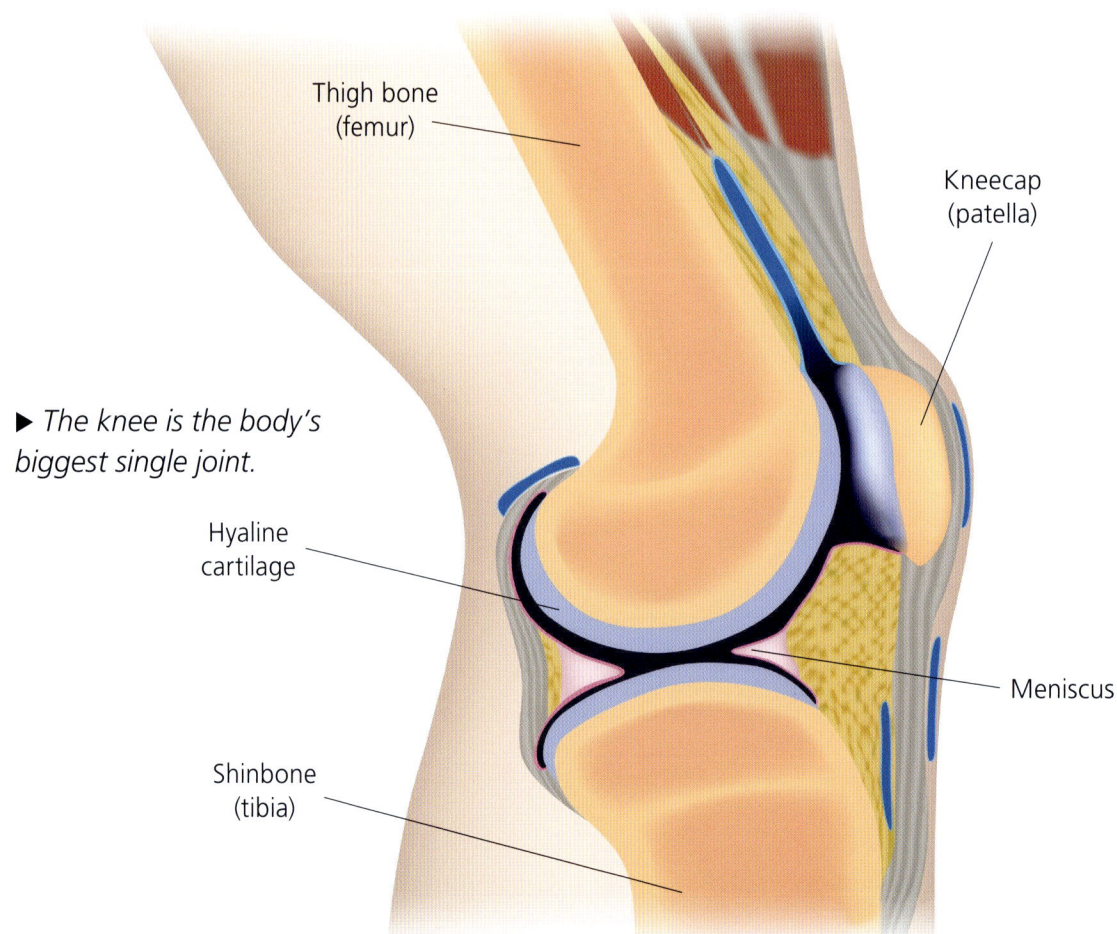

Thigh bone (femur)

Kneecap (patella)

▶ *The knee is the body's biggest single joint.*

Hyaline cartilage

Meniscus

Shinbone (tibia)

▲ Falling at an awkward angle, which can happen during sports such as rugby, may cause an injury – cartilage damage in the knee, for example.

- Elastic cartilage is very flexible and is used in your airways, nose and ears.

- Osteoarthritis is a condition that occurs when joint cartilage breaks down, making certain movements painful.

- Cartilage grows more rapidly than bone – a baby's skeleton is mostly cartilage, which gradually 'ossifies' (hardens into bone).

- Scientists can now create artificial cartilage that can be used to help repair damaged joints.

- Cartilage in the knee makes two dish-like shapes called menisci (singular: meniscus) between the thigh and lower leg bones.

DID YOU KNOW?
The word 'cartilage' comes from the Latin 'cartilago', which means gristle.

31

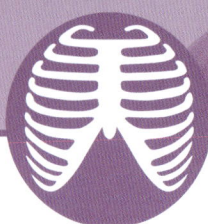

Tendons and ligaments

- Tendons are cords that tie a muscle to a bone or tie a muscle to another muscle.

- Most tendons are round, rope-like bundles of fibre. A few, such as the ones in the abdomen wall, are flat sheets called aponeuroses.

- Tendon fibres are made from a rubbery substance called collagen.

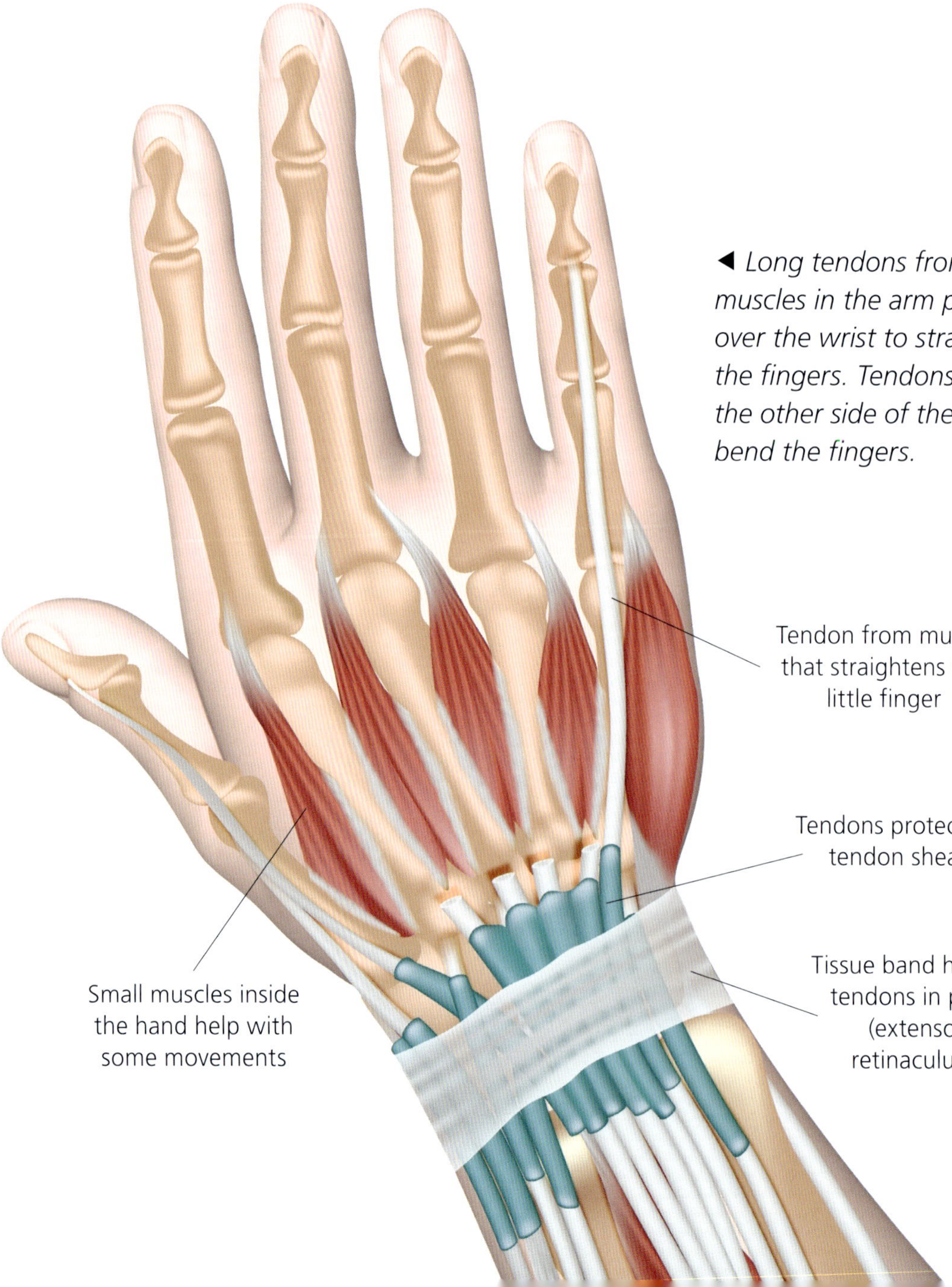

◄ *Long tendons from muscles in the arm pass over the wrist to straighten the fingers. Tendons on the other side of the hand bend the fingers.*

Tendon from muscle that straightens the little finger

Tendons protected by tendon sheaths

Tissue band holding tendons in place (extensor retinaculum)

Small muscles inside the hand help with some movements

► *Tendons provide a link between muscle and bone. They prevent muscles from tearing when they are put under strain.*

- Your fingers are moved mainly by muscles in the forearm, which are connected to the fingers by long tendons.

- The Achilles tendon pulls up your heel at the back.

- Ligaments are cords attached to bones on either side of a joint. They strengthen the joint.

- Ligaments also support various organs, including the liver, bladder and uterus (womb).

- Women's breasts are held in place by bundles of ligaments.

- Ligaments are made up of bundles of tough collagen and a stretchy substance called elastin.

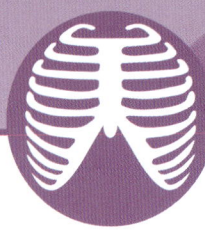

Muscles

- Muscles are special fibres that contract (tighten) and relax to move parts of the body.

- Muscles give our bodies their different shapes and help to hold the body upright.

- Most muscles attach to bones using tendons and most muscles cross over a joint so that they can move the joint.

- There are three types of muscle – skeletal, smooth and heart muscle.

- Most of the muscle in the body is skeletal muscle. There are around 640 skeletal muscles and they make up about half of your weight.

- Your body's longest muscle is the sartorius, on the inner thigh.

- The widest muscle is the external oblique, which runs around the side of the upper body.

- The biggest muscle is the gluteus maximus in each of your buttocks (of the bottom).

- The shortest muscle is the stapedius, which attaches to the stapes in the middle ear – the tiniest bone of the body.

DID YOU KNOW?
Your tongue is made up of eight muscles: four paired 'intrinsic' and four paired 'extrinsic' muscles.

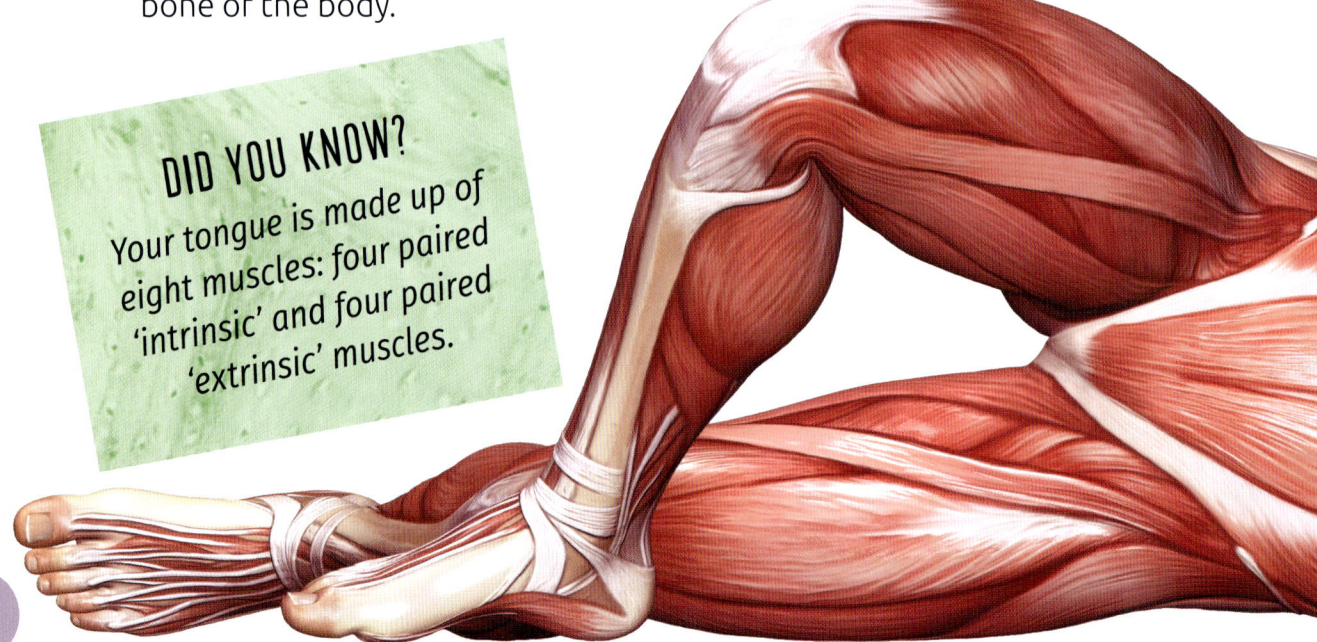

Muscle movement

- Most muscles are long and thin and they work by contracting (making themselves shorter) – sometimes contracting by up to half their length in response to signals from the brain.

- The stripes in skeletal muscle are alternating bands of filaments of two substances – actin and myosin.

- When one muscle contracts it pulls on the joint, creating movement. The muscle on the other side of the joint will be relaxed.

- To move the joint back to its original position, the contracted muscle relaxes and the opposing muscle contracts.

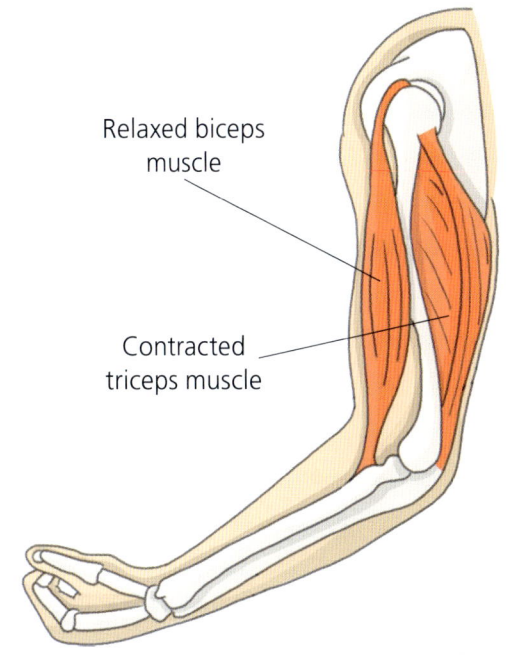

Relaxed biceps muscle

Contracted triceps muscle

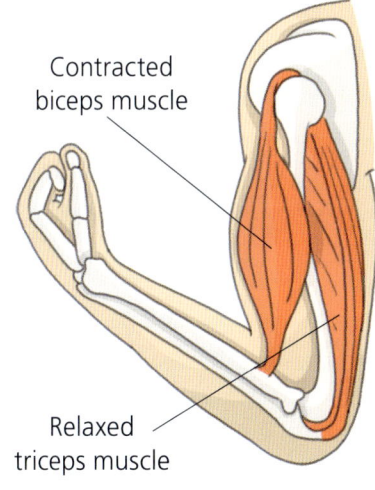

Contracted biceps muscle

Relaxed triceps muscle

▲ *The biceps and triceps muscles in your upper arm work in conjunction to pull your forearm one way, then the other.*

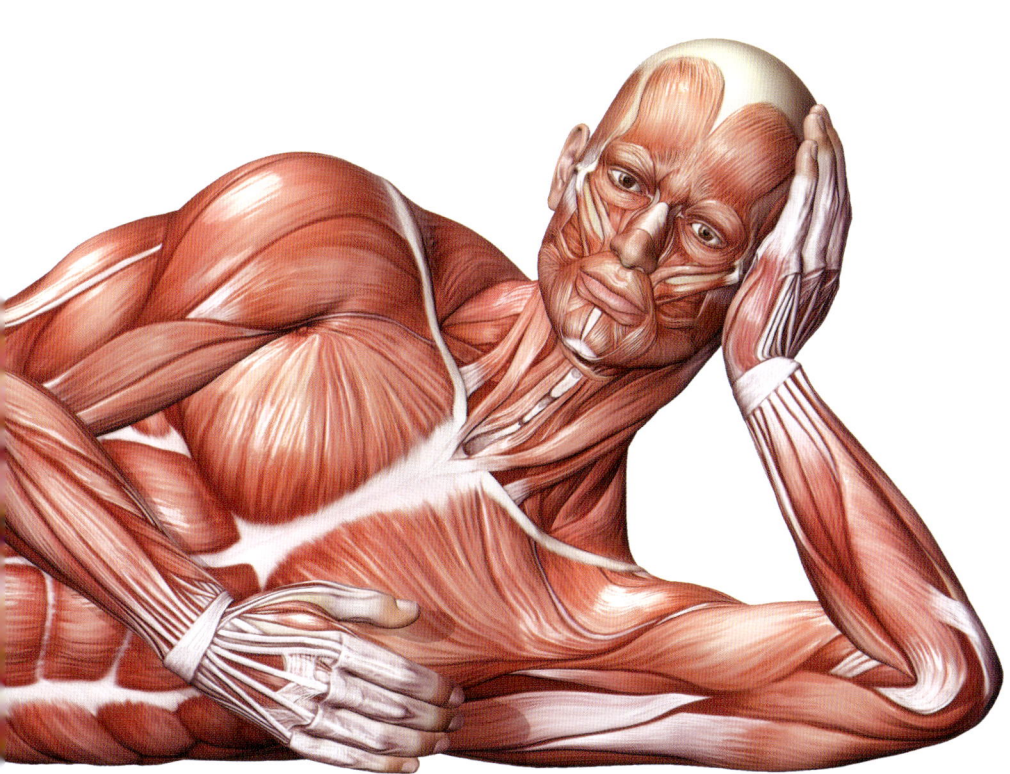

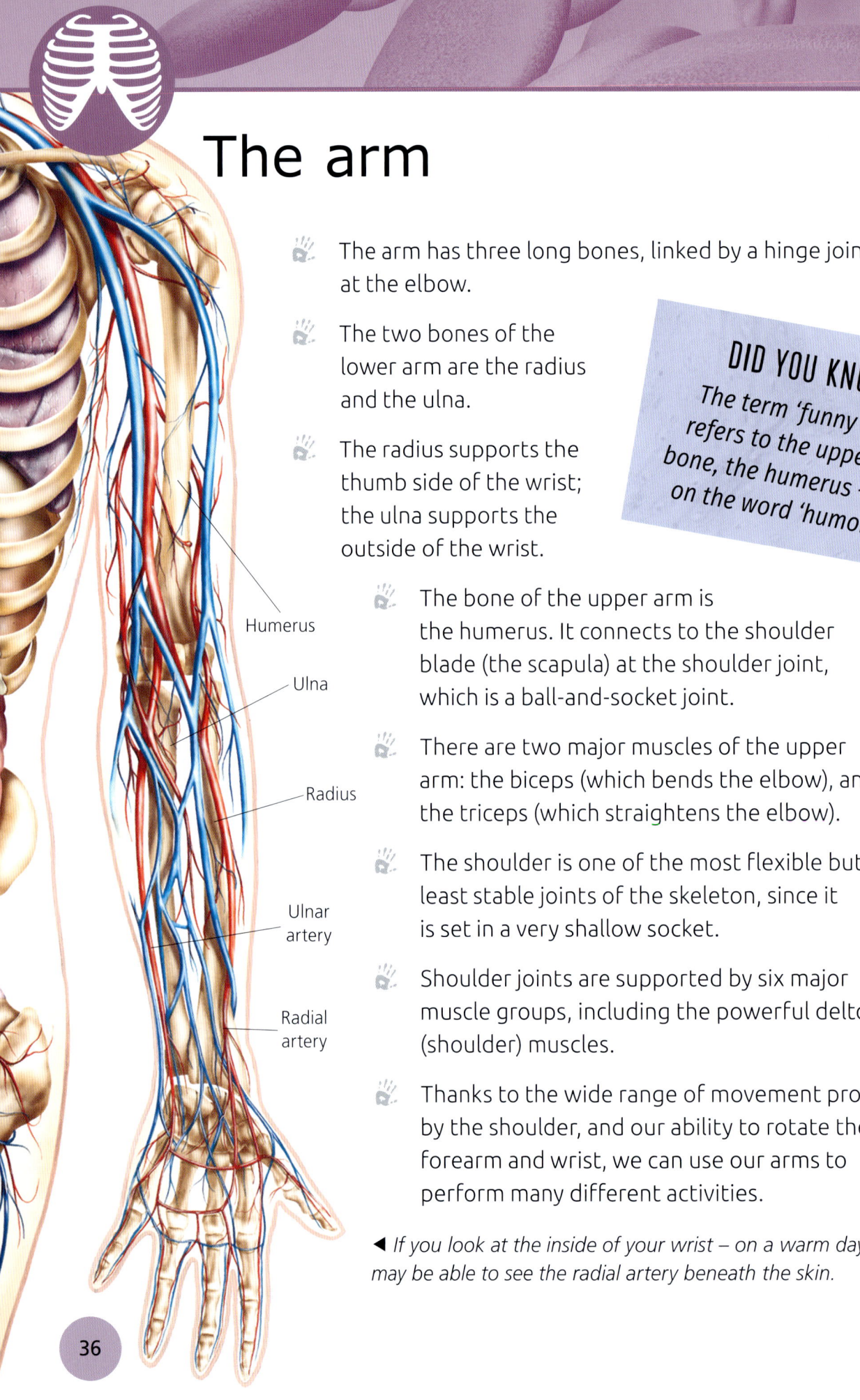

The arm

- The arm has three long bones, linked by a hinge joint at the elbow.

- The two bones of the lower arm are the radius and the ulna.

- The radius supports the thumb side of the wrist; the ulna supports the outside of the wrist.

- The bone of the upper arm is the humerus. It connects to the shoulder blade (the scapula) at the shoulder joint, which is a ball-and-socket joint.

- There are two major muscles of the upper arm: the biceps (which bends the elbow), and the triceps (which straightens the elbow).

- The shoulder is one of the most flexible but least stable joints of the skeleton, since it is set in a very shallow socket.

- Shoulder joints are supported by six major muscle groups, including the powerful deltoid (shoulder) muscles.

- Thanks to the wide range of movement provided by the shoulder, and our ability to rotate the forearm and wrist, we can use our arms to perform many different activities.

Humerus

Ulna

Radius

Ulnar artery

Radial artery

◄ *If you look at the inside of your wrist – on a warm day – you may be able to see the radial artery beneath the skin.*

36

The hand

- The hand has 27 bones, including the carpals (wrist bones), the metacarpals (hand bones) and the phalanges (finger bones).

- There are no strong muscles in the hand. When you grip firmly, most of the power comes from muscles in the lower arm.

- Humans and other primates, such as monkeys, have opposable thumbs. This means our thumbs can touch the tips of the fingers on the same hand.

- There are more nerve endings in the hand than anywhere else in the body. The fingertips are especially sensitive.

- Between 70 and 80 per cent of people are right-handed, giving them more coordination in their right hand than in their left.

- In the past, children who were left-handed were forced to write with their right hand. Even today, most tools, instruments and devices are made for right-handed people.

▶ *The intricate network of bones in your hands enables you to perform delicate and complex movements such as writing or playing a musical instrument.*

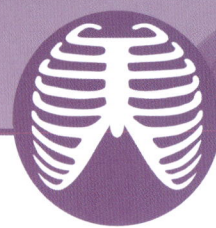

The leg

- The leg is made up of three long bones, linked by a hinge joint at the knee.

- The femur (thigh bone) is the body's longest bone.

- The femur connects to the pelvis at the hip joint (a ball-and-socket joint).

- The hip is one of the strongest joints in the body. The ball at the end of the femur sits in a very deep cup in the pelvis, making it almost impossible to dislocate it.

- The two bones of the lower leg are the tibia and fibula.

- The tibia is the main 'shinbone' at the front of the leg; the fibula lies to the outer side and slightly behind.

- The muscles of the leg are strong enough to enable us to sit, stand, walk and run. The largest muscle in the body, the gluteus maximus, is used for stepping or standing up.

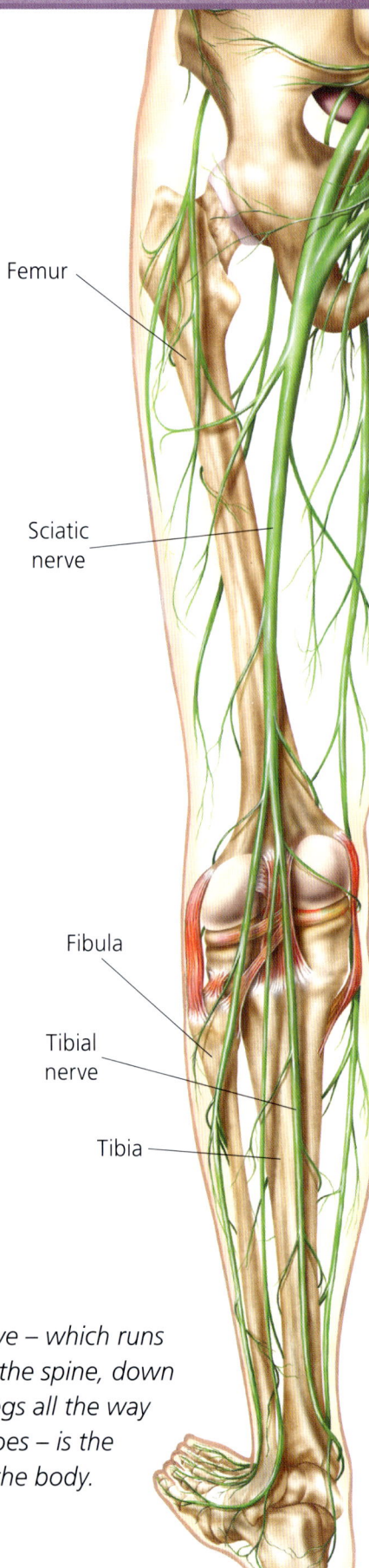

Femur

Sciatic nerve

Fibula

Tibial nerve

Tibia

DID YOU KNOW?
In anatomy, the word 'leg' actually refers only to the part of the leg between the knee and ankle.

▶ *The sciatic nerve – which runs from the base of the spine, down the back of the legs all the way to the heel and toes – is the longest nerve in the body.*

The foot

- The foot is made up of 26 bones, including the tarsals (or ankle bones), the metatarsals (or foot bones) and the phalanges (or toe bones).

- The ankle and part of the foot nearest the ankle contain seven bones called the tarsal bones.

- Movement of the ankle, foot and toes mostly comes from muscles in the lower leg, linked to the bones of the foot by long tendons.

- We use our feet and toes to aid balance. The big toes are especially important: without them, it would be much harder to walk and stand upright.

- Feet usually have an arch in the middle formed by the shape of the bones and strong tendons. Someone with no arch is said to have 'flat feet'.

- The world record for the most fingers and toes in one person is 25, with 12 fingers and 13 toes.

▲ Ballerinas who dance 'en pointe' (up on the toes) wear special shoes that help to support their feet.

▼ The 26 bones of each foot provide support for the weight of the body.

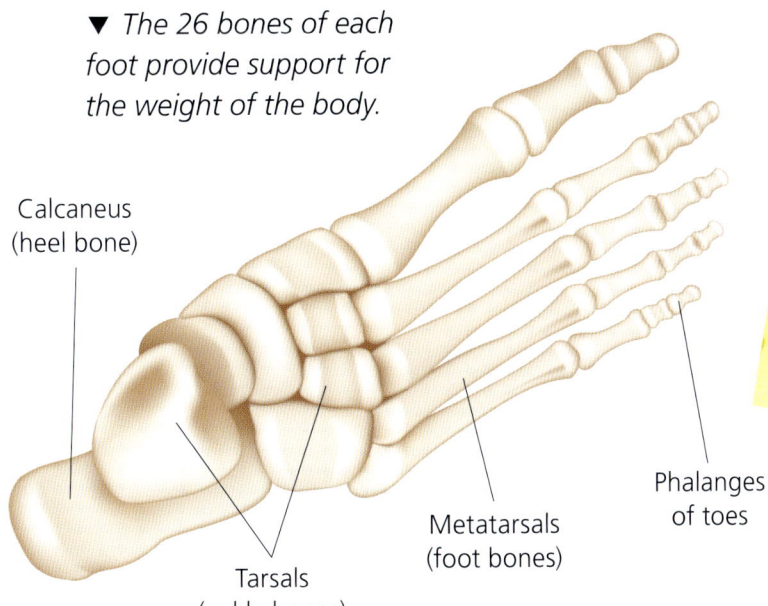

Calcaneus (heel bone)

Tarsals (ankle bones)

Metatarsals (foot bones)

Phalanges of toes

DID YOU KNOW?
The foot contains dozens of muscles, tendons and ligaments.

39

The nervous system

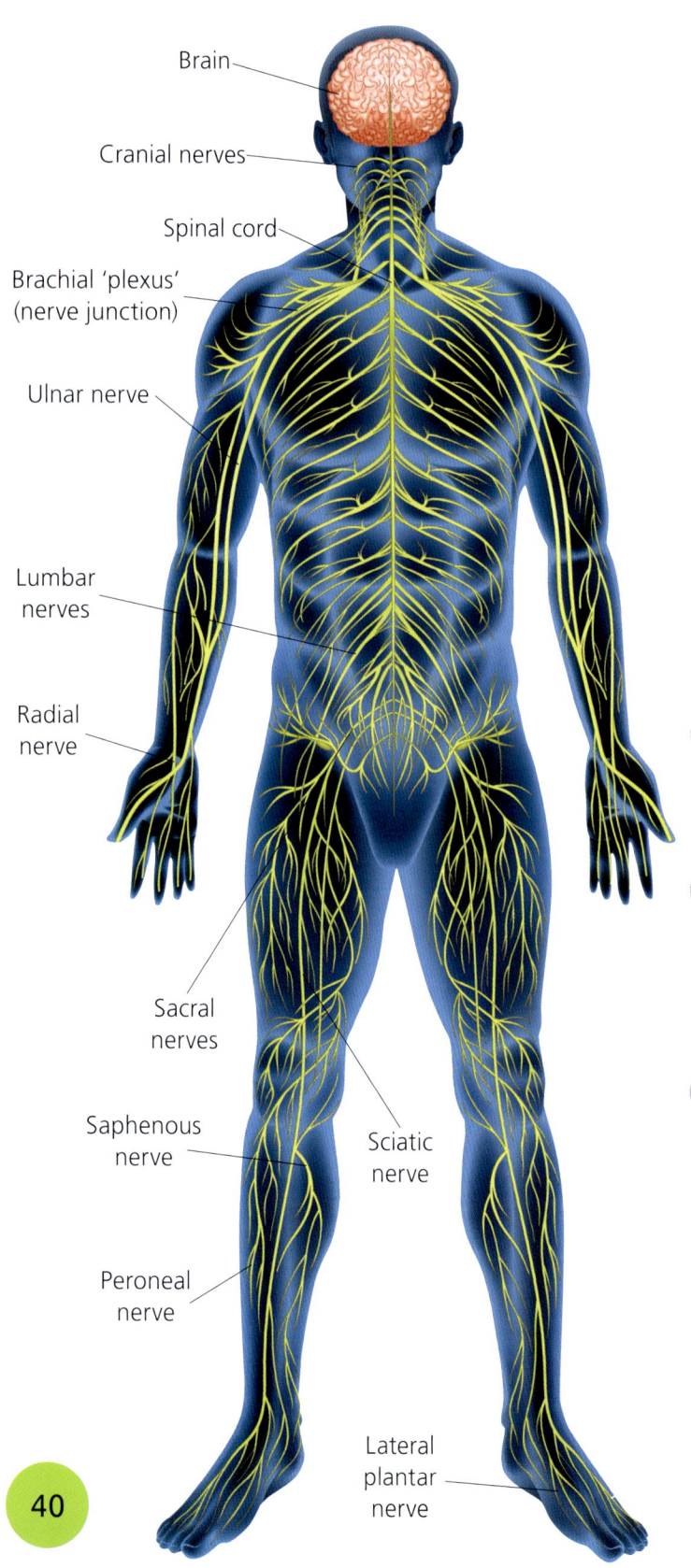

Brain

Cranial nerves

Spinal cord

Brachial 'plexus'
(nerve junction)

Ulnar nerve

Lumbar
nerves

Radial
nerve

Sacral
nerves

Saphenous
nerve

Sciatic
nerve

Peroneal
nerve

Lateral
plantar
nerve

- The nervous system is your body's communication and control system, made up of nerves and the brain.

- Nerves are your body's 'hotlines', carrying instant messages from the brain to every organ and muscle – and transmitting back an endless stream of data to the brain.

- The nervous system is divided into two parts – the central nervous system and the peripheral nervous system.

- The central nervous system (CNS) consists of the brain and spinal cord.

- Peripheral nervous system (PNS) consists of the nerves that branch out from the CNS to the rest of the body.

- Some PNS nerves are as wide as your thumb. The longest is the sciatic nerve.

◄ *The nervous system is an incredibly intricate network of nerves linking the brain to every part of the body.*

▲ *The process of having brain waves measured is called electroencephalography (or EEG). It is used to help diagnose nervous system disorders.*

The PNS can be divided into nerves that control 'voluntary' actions, such as walking, and those that control 'involuntary' body functions.

The autonomic nervous system (ANS) is part of the PNS. It controls all internal body processes – such as your heart rate, digestion and breathing – automatically, without you even being aware of it.

The ANS is split into two complementary (balancing) parts – the sympathetic and the parasympathetic. The sympathetic system speeds up body processes when they need to be more active, such as when the body is exercising. The parasympathetic slows them down.

Nerves can be divided into motor nerves, which carry messages from the brain to muscles to control movement, and sensory nerves, which carry messages from the body's sensory receptors to the brain.

In many places, sensory nerves run alongside motor nerves.

Central nervous system

- The central nervous system (CNS) consists of the brain and the spinal cord (the nerves of the spine).

- It is responsible for collecting information from all the other nerves in the body, processing data and sending out appropriate responses.

- The CNS contains billions of densely packed interneurons, nerve cells with very short connecting 'axons' (tails).

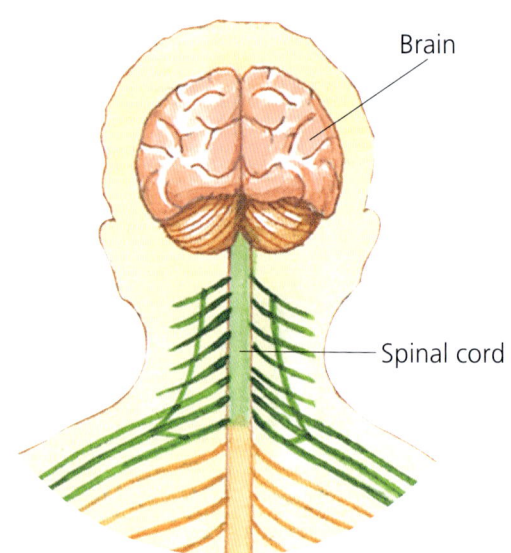

Brain

Spinal cord

- A surrounding bath of liquid – called cerebrospinal fluid – cushions the CNS from damage.

- There are 43 pairs of nerves branching off from the CNS.

- There are 12 pairs of cranial nerves and 31 pairs of spinal nerves.

- Cranial nerves are the 12 pairs of nerves that branch off from the CNS out of the brain.

- Spinal nerves are the 31 pairs of nerves that branch off from the spinal cord.

- The spinal nerves are made up of eight cervical nerve pairs, 12 thoracic pairs, five lumbar pairs, five sacral pairs and one coccyx pair.

- Many spinal nerves join up just outside the spine in five 'spaghetti junctions' known as plexuses.

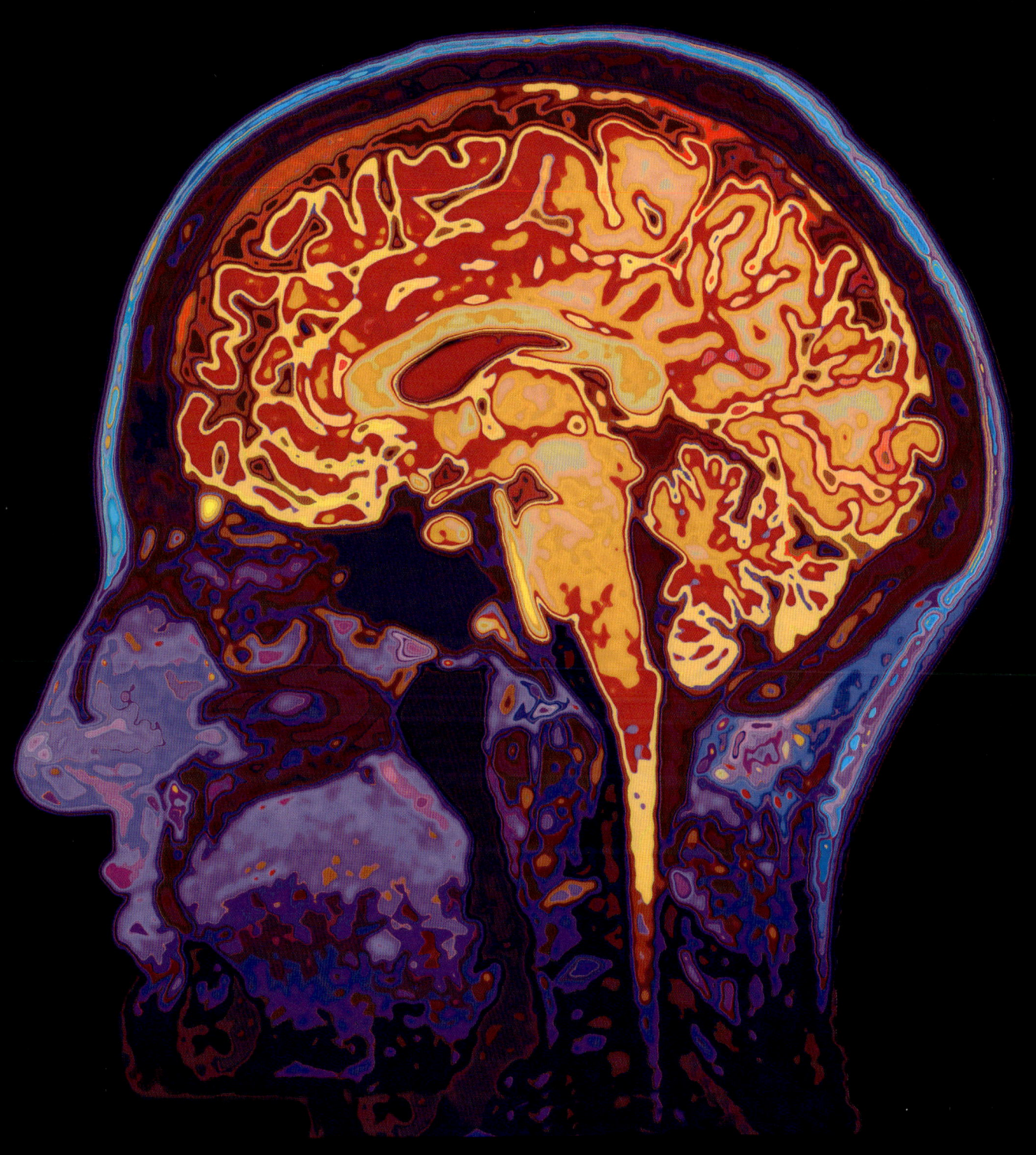

▲ *The brain's cortex (outer layer) is only 5 mm thick – but, if flattened out, it would cover an area almost as big as an office desk. It contains at least 50 billion nerve cells.*

Nerve cells

- Nerves are made of very specialized cells called neurons.

- Neurons are spider-shaped with a nucleus at the centre, lots of branching threads called dendrites – and a winding tail called an axon, which can be up to one metre long.

- Neurons link up like beads on a string to make up the nervous system.

- Most cells are short-lived and replaced by new ones. Neurons, however, are very long-lasting – some never need to be replaced.

- Nerve signals travel as electrical pulses, each pulse lasting about 0.001 seconds.

- When nerves are resting there are extra sodium ions (with a positive electrical charge) on the outside of the nerve cell, and extra negative ions inside the cell.

- When a nerve fires, little gates open in the cell wall all along the nerve, and positive ions rush in to join the negative ions. This creates an electrical pulse.

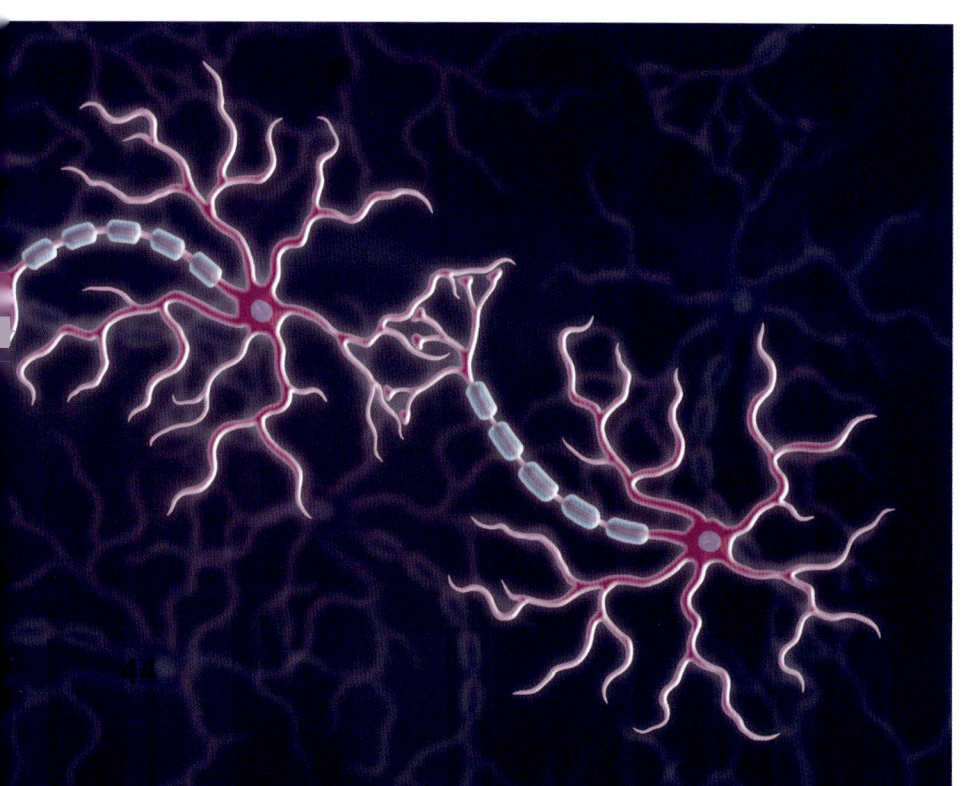

◄ Nerve cells, or neurons, are the 'wires' of the body's nervous system. They carry messages within, to and from the central nervous system along fine branches (dendrites) and long tails (axons).

Synapses

- Synapses are the very tiny gaps between nerve cells.

- When a nerve signal moves from one nerve cell to another, it must be transmitted (sent) across the synapse by special chemicals called neurotransmitters.

- Droplets of neurotransmitter are released into the synapse whenever a nerve signal arrives.

- As the droplets of neurotransmitter lock on to the receiving nerve's receptors, they fire the signal onwards.

- Each receptor only reacts to certain neurotransmitters.

- Sometimes, several signals must arrive before enough neurotransmitter is released to fire the receiving nerve.

- More than 40 neurotransmitter chemicals have been identified.

- Dopamine is a neurotransmitter that works in the parts of the brain that control movement and learning. Parkinson's disease may develop when the nerves that produce dopamine break down.

- Serotonin is a neurotransmitter that is linked to mood, sleeping and waking up.

- Acetylcholine is a neurotransmitter that may be involved in memory, and also in the nerves that control muscle movement.

> **DID YOU KNOW?**
> It is thought that an adult human might have more than 100 trillion synapses in his or her brain.

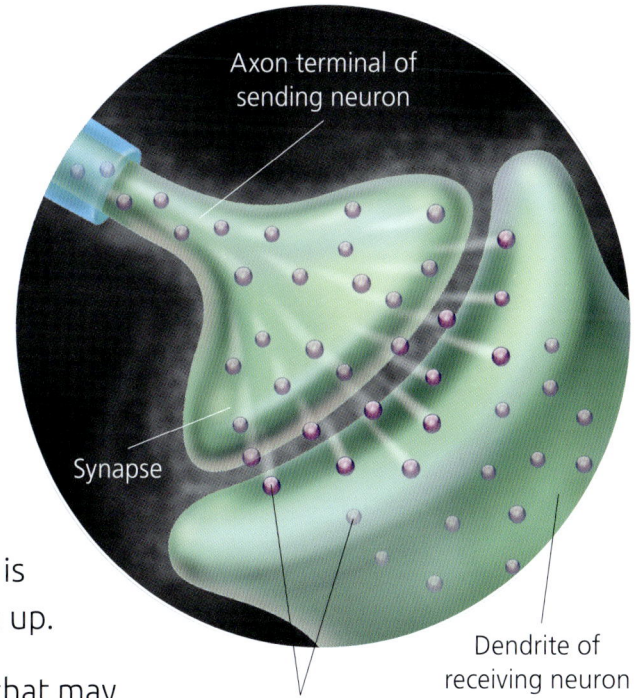

Axon terminal of sending neuron

Synapse

Neurotransmitters

Dendrite of receiving neuron

45

The brain

- The human brain is made up of more than 100 billion nerve cells called neurons.

- Each neuron is connected to as many as 25,000 other neurons – so the brain has trillions and trillions of different pathways for nerve signals.

- As well as controlling day-to-day actions and responses, the brain enables us to think, learn, understand and create.

- The main part of the brain is called the cerebrum and is divided into two halves. The left half controls the right side of the body, while the right half controls the left side of the body.

- At the base of the brain, the cerebellum controls your co-ordination and fine movement.

◄ *Taking the top off the skull shows the brain to be a soggy, pinky-grey mass, which looks rather like a giant walnut.*

46

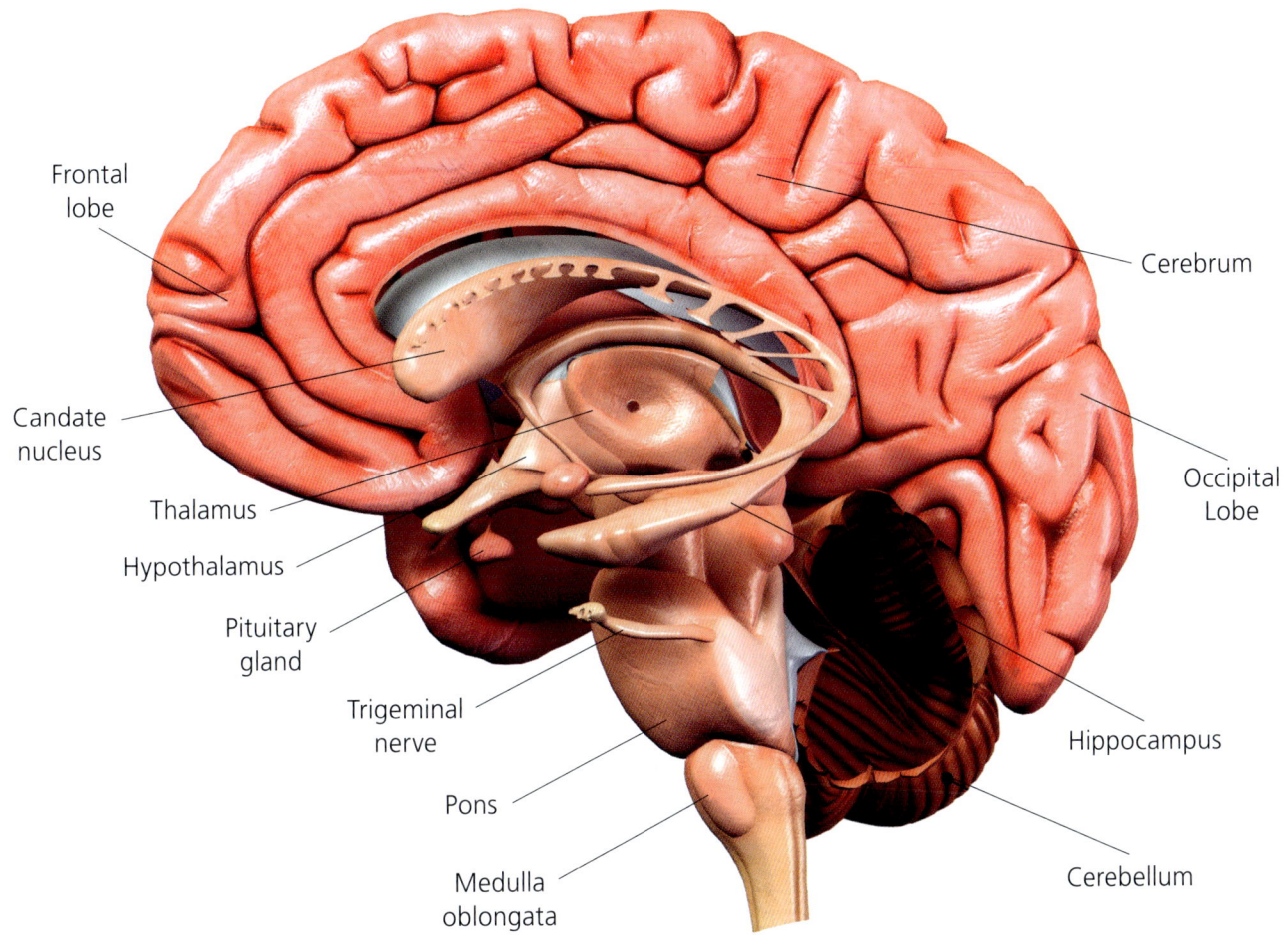

Frontal lobe

Cerebrum

Candate nucleus

Thalamus

Hypothalamus

Pituitary gland

Trigeminal nerve

Pons

Medulla oblongata

Occipital Lobe

Hippocampus

Cerebellum

▲ *In this illustration, the right hemisphere (half) of the cerebrum is shown in pink, surrounding the regions that control basic drives such as hunger, thirst and anger.*

Girls' brains make up approximately 2.5 per cent of their body weight, on average, while boys' brains make up 2 per cent of their weight.

About 0.85 litres of blood shoots through your brain every minute. The brain may be as little as 2 per cent of your overall weight, but it demands 12 to 15 per cent of your blood supply.

The cerebral cortex

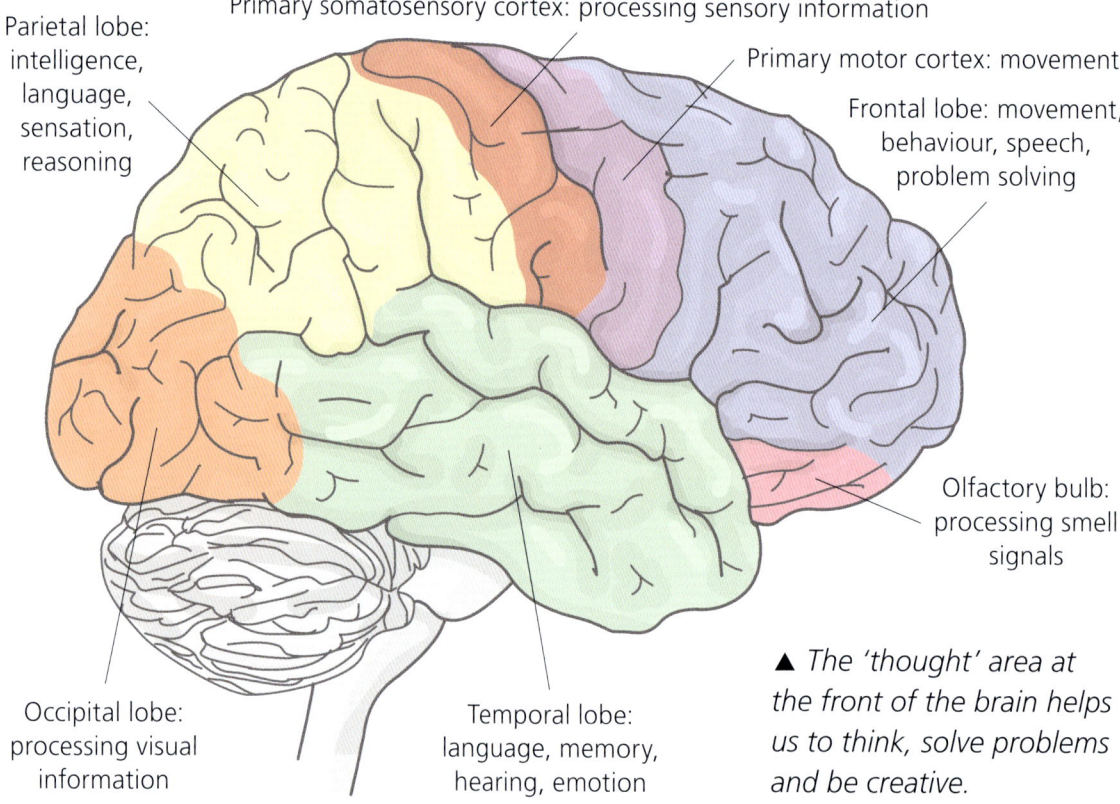

Parietal lobe: intelligence, language, sensation, reasoning

Primary somatosensory cortex: processing sensory information

Primary motor cortex: movement

Frontal lobe: movement, behaviour, speech, problem solving

Olfactory bulb: processing smell signals

Occipital lobe: processing visual information

Temporal lobe: language, memory, hearing, emotion

▲ *The 'thought' area at the front of the brain helps us to think, solve problems and be creative.*

- A cortex is the outer layer of any organ, such as the brain or the kidney.

- The cerebral cortex is a layer of interconnected nerve cells around the outside of the brain. It is also known as 'grey matter'.

- The cerebral cortex is responsible for 'higher-level' functions including conscious thoughts and actions.

- Many signals from the senses are registered in the cerebral cortex.

- The visual cortex is located at the lower back region of the brain. It is the place where all the things you see are registered in the brain.

- The motor cortex sends out signals to muscles to make them move.

- A human brain has a cerebral cortex approximately 20 times larger than a monkey's and about 300 times bigger than a rat's.

The spinal cord

- The spinal cord is the bundle of nerves running down the middle of the backbone.

- It is the route for all nerve signals travelling between the brain and all the other regions of the body.

- The spinal cord can actually work independently of the brain, sending out responses to the muscles directly.

- The outside of the spinal cord, known as white matter, is composed of the long tails, or axons, of nerve cells. The inside of the spinal cord, known as grey matter, is made up of the main nerve bodies.

- Your spinal cord is about 43 cm long and one centimetre thick.

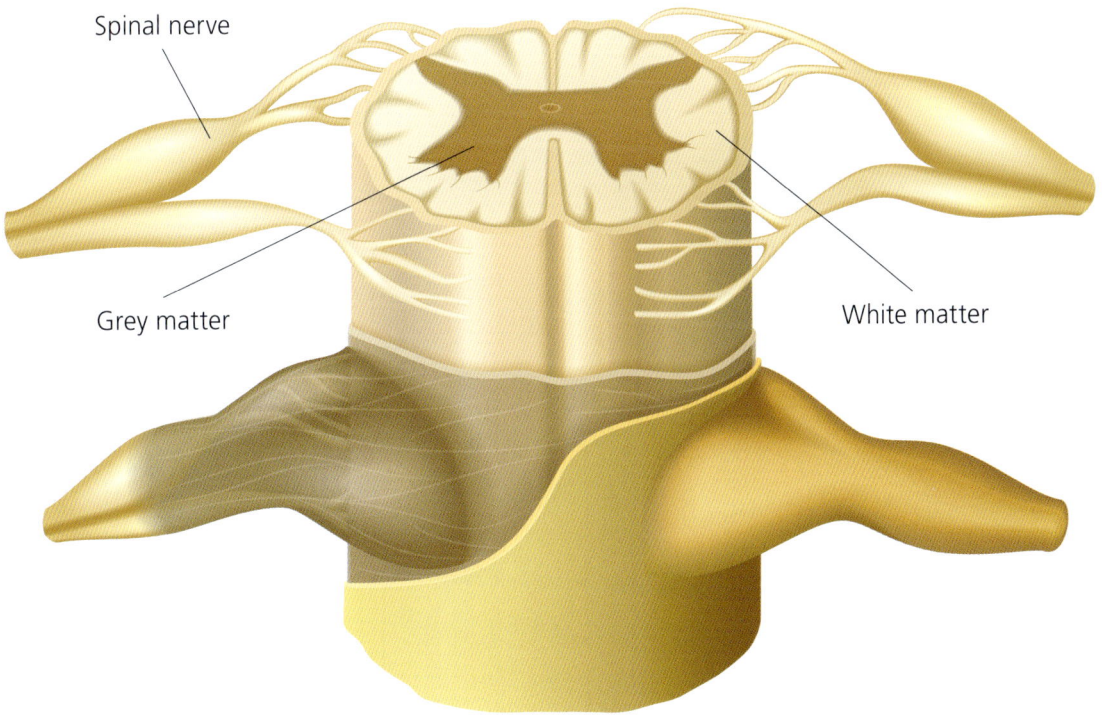

Spinal nerve

Grey matter

White matter

▲ *The spinal cord is encased in a 'tunnel' inside the spine – at the back of each vertebra. Nerves branch off to the body in pairs on either side.*

Peripheral nervous system

- The peripheral nervous system (PNS) consists of the 12 cranial nerves in the head and the 31 pairs of spinal nerves that branch off from the spinal cord.

- Several of the spinal nerves combine to form collections of nerves called nerve plexuses.

- Located in the head, the cervical plexus provides the nerves that supply the neck and shoulders.

- The plexus in the neck and upper arm is called the brachial plexus and supplies the arm and the upper back.

- Pins and needles occur when you pinch one of your peripheral nerves by sitting awkwardly or holding an arm or leg in a funny position for a long time.

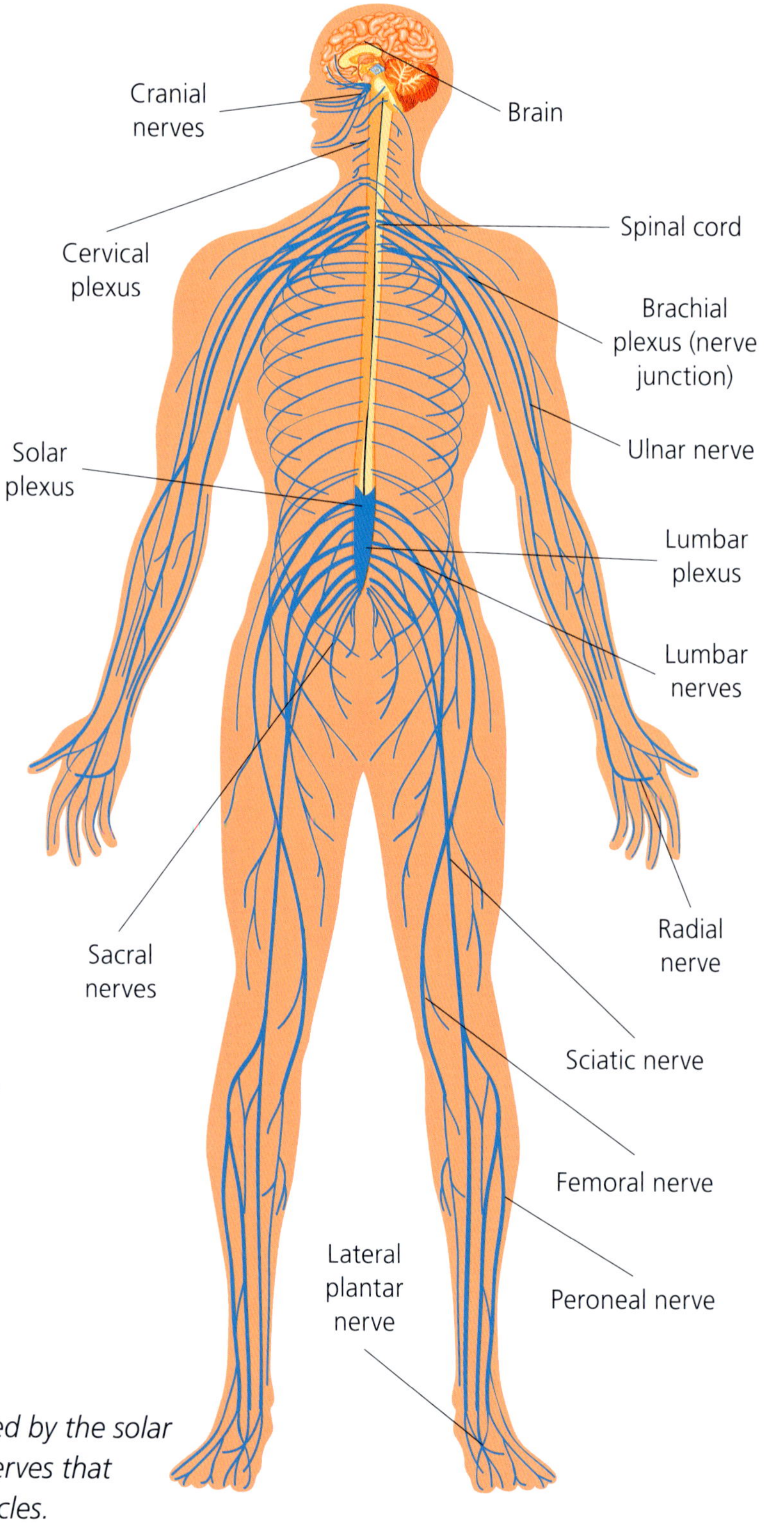

▶ Nerves in the abdomen are provided by the solar plexus. The lumbar plexus contains nerves that supply the abdomen and the leg muscles.

Cranial nerves

Brain

Cervical plexus

Spinal cord

Brachial plexus (nerve junction)

Ulnar nerve

Solar plexus

Lumbar plexus

Lumbar nerves

Sacral nerves

Radial nerve

Sciatic nerve

Femoral nerve

Lateral plantar nerve

Peroneal nerve

Cranial nerves

- There are 12 pairs of cranial nerves that emerge directly from the brain.

- The eyes are linked to the brain by the optic nerves, which carry visual data.

- The nose is linked to the brain by the olfactory nerves.

- The trigeminal nerves control chewing and receive sensations from the face.

- The facial nerves control your facial expression and carry information about your sense of taste to the brain.

- Balance and movement are aided by the vestibulocochlear nerve.

- The glossopharyngeal nerve also carries information about your sense of taste to the brain.

- The vagus nerve performs many functions, including the control of your heart rate and speech.

- Some of the movements of your neck and shoulders, such as shrugging, are controlled by the accessory nerves.

- The last nerve, the hypoglossal nerve, helps you to swallow and talk by controlling the tongue.

DID YOU KNOW?
Cranial means something to do with the skull. However, not all 'cranial' nerves go to the head.

▶ *The ability to smile is provided by the action of the facial nerve, which sends signals from the brain to the muscles of the face.*

51

Sensory nerves

▲ *We rely on sight more than our other senses, but to fully enjoy a fireworks display we need our olfactory (smelling) and auditory (hearing) senses as well.*

- Sensory nerves are the nerves that carry information to your brain from sense receptors all over your body.

- Sense receptors include the sense organs, such as the eyes, and receptors in the skin.

Massive bundles of sensory nerve cells form the nerves that link major senses – such as the eyes, ears and nose – to the brain.

Sense receptors are also located in the mouth, throat and in the lining of the internal organs.

In the skin, many sense receptors are simply 'free' – meaning they are exposed sensory nerve endings.

Free nerve endings are rather like the bare end of a wire. They respond to all kinds of skin sensation and are almost everywhere in your skin.

Most sensory nerves feed their signals to the somatosensory cortex (see page 48), which is a region situated around the top of the brain where sensations are registered.

In the middle of your brain, the egg-shaped thalamus serves as the 'relay station' for most of the incoming sensory information.

We can tell how strong a sensation is by how fast the sensory nerve fires signals to the brain – but, no matter how strong the sensation is, the nerve does not go on firing at the same rate and soon slows down.

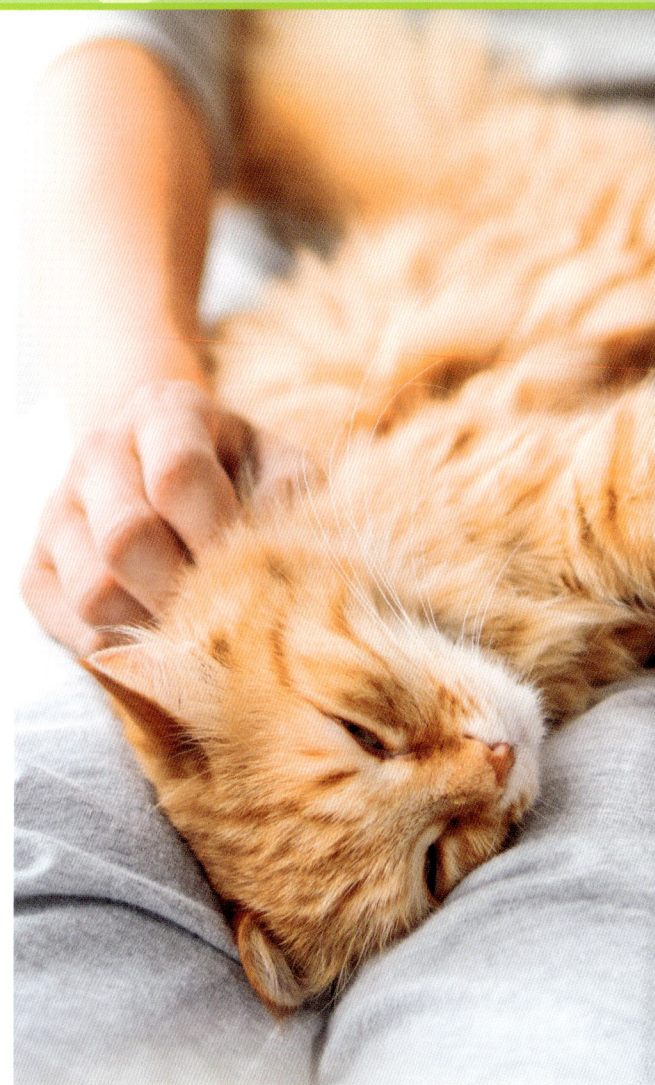

▲ Some of our most pleasant feelings, such as being hugged or stroked, are sent to the brain by the sensory nerves.

DID YOU KNOW?
Sense receptors are in all regions of skin, but some areas, such as your face, have more than others.

53

The nose

- You use your nose to smell and to breathe in air.

- The nose is made up of skin and cartilage attached to the ethmoid bone of the skull. The two nostrils are separated by a piece of cartilage called the nasal septum.

- We breathe in through our nostrils, which open up into the nasal cavity – a large space between the mouth and the brain.

- The nasal cavity cells can detect different scents and smells.

- The human nose can tell the difference between more than 10,000 different chemicals, known as odorants.

- Hairs within the nose trap dust and other particles, preventing them from entering your airways.

DID YOU KNOW?
In some people, sudden exposure to bright light causes sneezing.

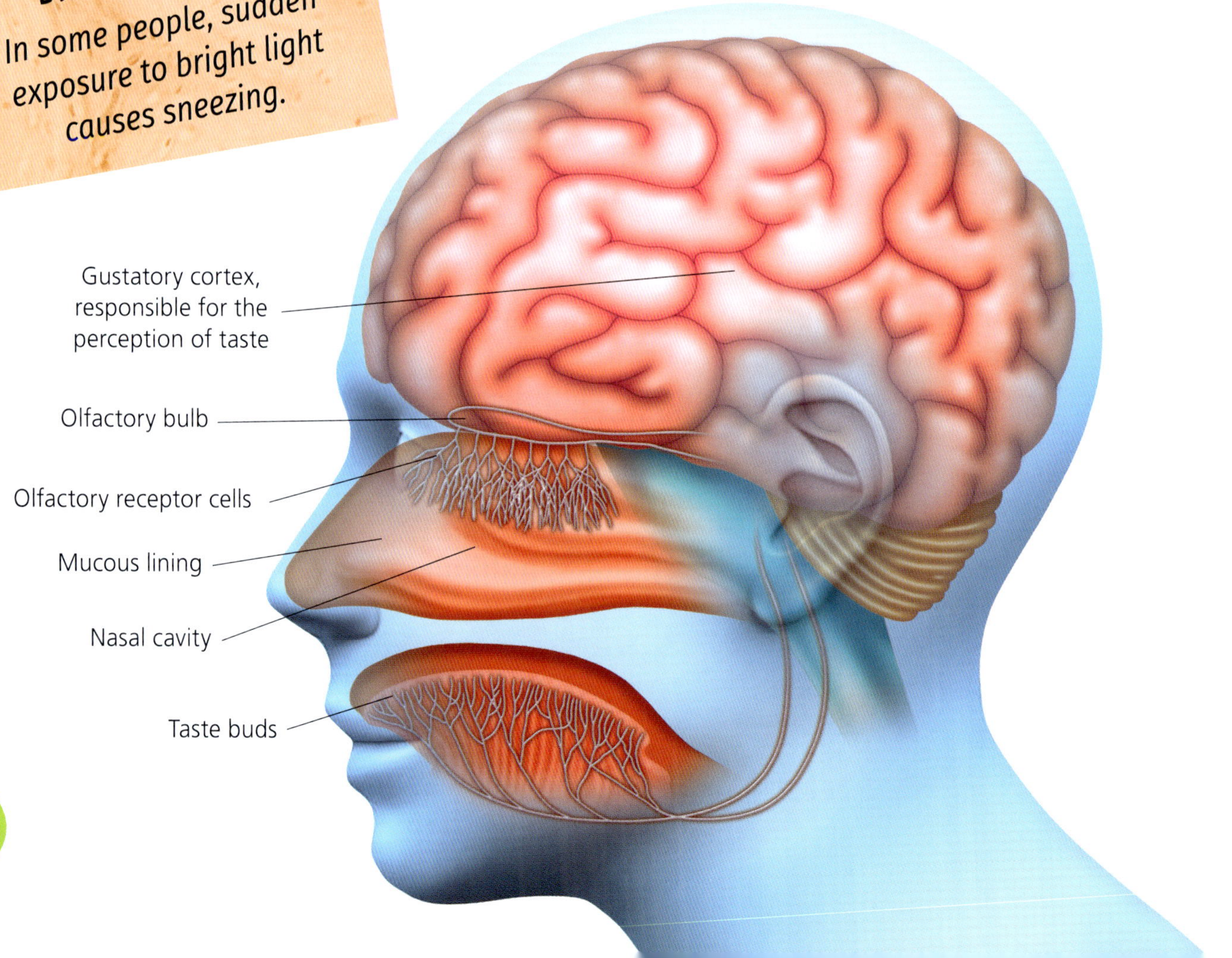

Gustatory cortex, responsible for the perception of taste

Olfactory bulb

Olfactory receptor cells

Mucous lining

Nasal cavity

Taste buds

Smell

Smells are scent molecules that are taken into your nose by breathed-in air. A particular smell may be noticeable even when just a single scent molecule is mixed in with millions of air molecules.

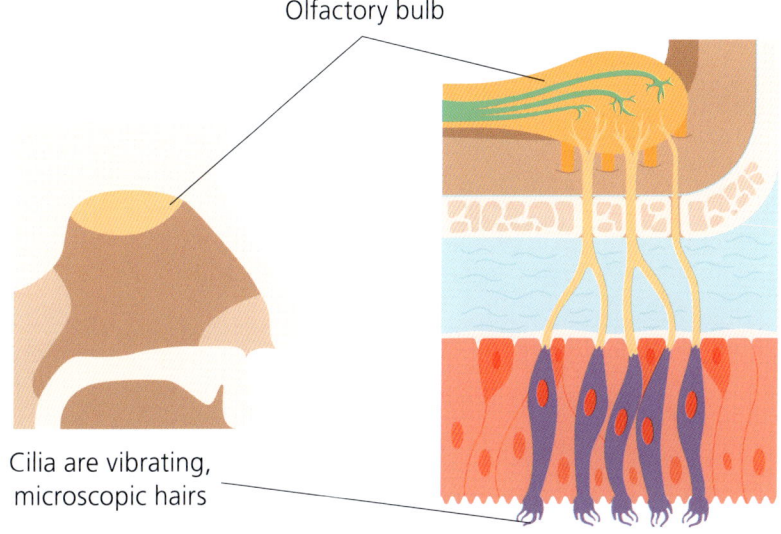

Olfactory bulb

Cilia are vibrating, microscopic hairs

▲ *Olfactory cells have micro-hairs facing into the nasal chamber – for detecting smell particles.*

Inside the nose, scent molecules are picked up by a patch of scent-sensitive cells known as the olfactory epithelium.

The olfactory epithelium contains more than 25 million receptor cells.

Each of the receptor cells in the olfactory epithelium has up to 20 or so scent-detecting hairs called cilia.

When they are triggered by scent molecules, the cilia send signals to a cluster of nerves called the olfactory bulb, which then sends messages to the part of the brain that recognizes smell.

The part of the brain that deals with smell is closely linked to the parts that deal with memories and emotions. This may be why smells can often trigger vivid memories connected with them.

DID YOU KNOW?
The human sense of smell is relatively poor – bears can smell food from many kilometres away.

Taste

The sense of taste is the crudest of our five senses, giving us less information about the world than the other main senses.

Taste is triggered by certain chemicals in food, which dissolve in the saliva in your mouth and then come into contact with specialised taste receptor cells in the mouth and throat.

Taste buds are receptor cells found around tiny bumps called papillae on the surface of the tongue and also in your throat.

As well as taste, the tongue can detect the texture and temperature of food.

Your sense of taste works closely together with your sense of smell to make food flavours more interesting.

Strong tastes, such as those in spicy food, rely less on the sense of smell than on pain-sensitive nerve endings in the tongue.

▼ *This powerful microscope picture of the surface of the tongue shows the papillae (highlighted in pink) that contain the taste buds.*

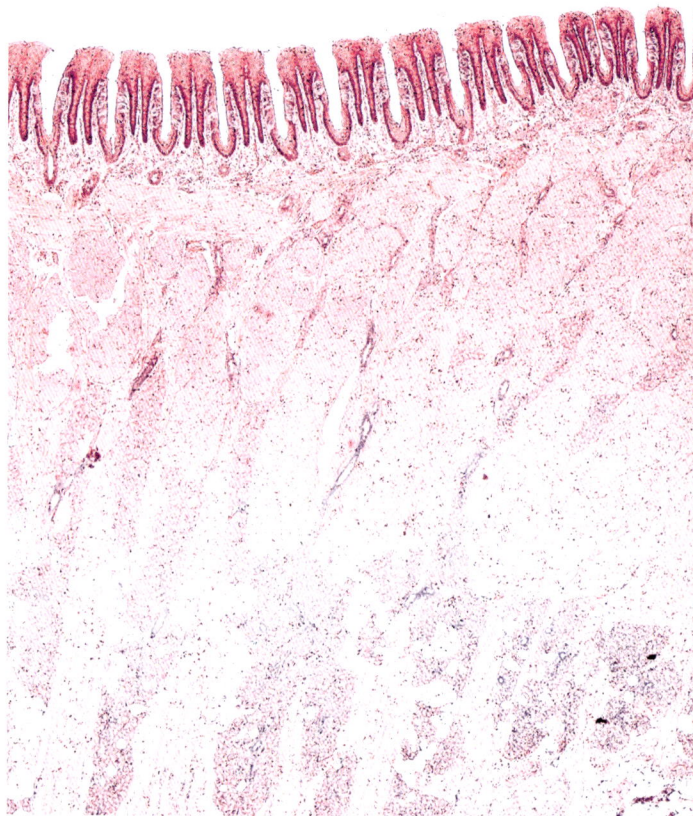

DID YOU KNOW?
There are currently five distinctive, recognised tastes: umami (or savoury), as well as sweet, salty, bitter and sour.

Touch

- Touch sensors in our skin help to relay information to the brain, enabling us to feel.

- There are several aspects to touch – we feel light and deep pressure, hot, cold and pain.

- We use touch to learn about our surroundings and carry out everyday activities such as holding objects.

- Without our sense of touch, we would not know how much pressure to use when picking something up. We might drop things or squeeze them too tightly, causing them to break.

- Touch also warns us of danger. We feel pain if we touch something too hot or too cold – and we learn to move away from the danger.

- For blind and partially sighted people, touch is particularly important in helping them to recognise their environment. Many blind people learn to read Braille, so that they can recognise words through touch.

▶ *This magnified view shows touch sensors beneath the skin.*

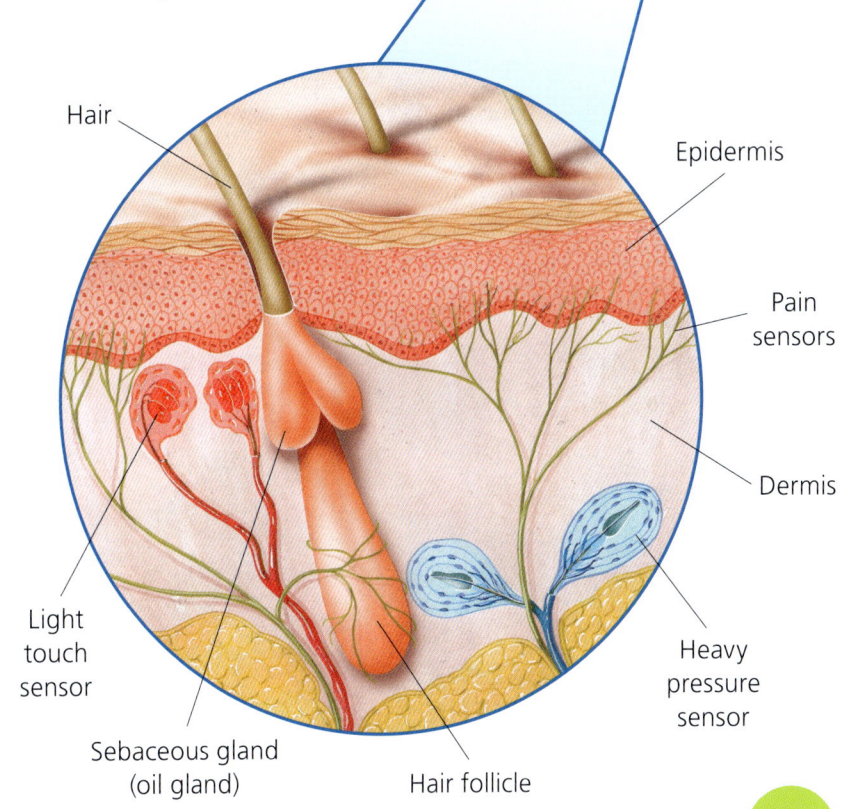

Hair

Epidermis

Pain sensors

Dermis

Light touch sensor

Heavy pressure sensor

Sebaceous gland (oil gland)

Hair follicle

57

The eye

- Your eyes are tough orbs that are filled with a jellylike substance called vitreous humour.

- The eyes are protected by bony sockets in the skull, while eyelids and eyelashes help to shield their surfaces from dust and dirt.

- The outer layer of the eye, the sclera, helps to preserve the eye's shape.

- The cornea is a thin, glassy dish across the front of each eye. It allows light rays to pass through the pupil and into the lens.

- The iris is the coloured, muscular ring around the pupil. It contracts (narrows) in bright light and relaxes (widens) when in dim conditions.

- The lens is just behind the pupil. It focuses the picture of the world onto the back of the eye, where the retina is located.

- The back of the eye is lined with millions of light-sensitive cells. This lining is the retina, which registers the picture and sends signals to the brain via the optic nerve.

- Strong muscles that surround each eye enable us to move our eyeballs in different directions.

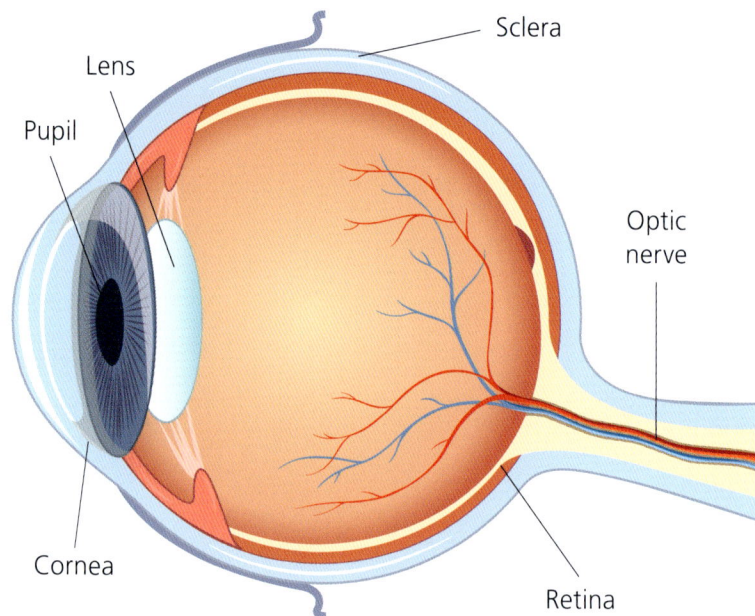

▲ *Vitreous humour in the main body of the eye holds the eye's spherical shape.*

DID YOU KNOW?
The picture received by your retina seems broad and accurate – yet it is upside down and just a few millimetres wide.

Vision

- When you look at an object, light from the object hits the cornea at the front of your eye and is bent by the cornea onto the lens.

- The lens in the eye focuses the light onto the retina at the back of the eye. The most sensitive part of the retina is called the fovea.

- The cells in the retina collect the information and send signals to the brain, which interprets the signals as images.

- There are two kinds of light-sensitive cell in the retina – rods and cones. Rods are very sensitive and work even in dim light, but they cannot detect colours. Cones respond to colour.

- Each of your eyes gives you a slightly different view. The brain combines them to create an impression of depth and 3D solidity.

- People who have difficulty seeing distant objects are known as short-sighted. People who have difficulty focusing on nearby objects are called long-sighted.

- Short and long sight occurs when the light from the object you are looking at is not properly focused on the retina by the lens in the eye.

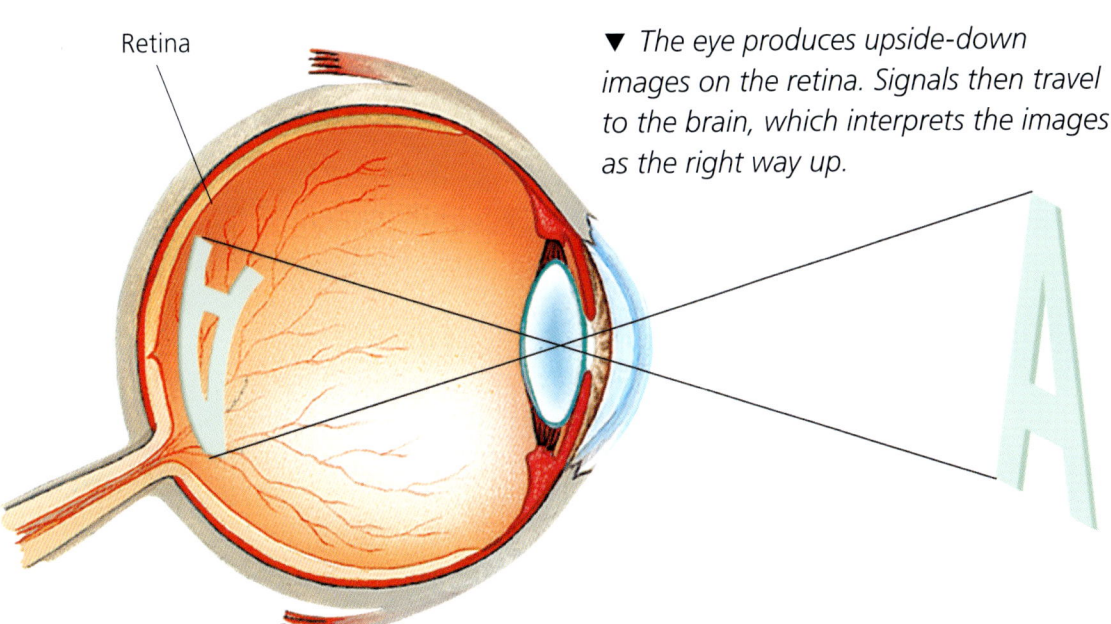

Retina

▼ *The eye produces upside-down images on the retina. Signals then travel to the brain, which interprets the images as the right way up.*

The ear

- Ears aren't just for hearing; they also assist us with our balance and keeping our posture (our standing or sitting position).

- The ear has three parts: the outer ear (the part you can see and the canal that leads to the eardrum), the middle ear and the inner ear.

- Pinnae (singular: pinna) are the ear flaps you can see on the side of your head. They are funnels for collecting and amplifying sounds.

- The channel leading from the pinna is the ear canal. Glands in the ear canal produce ear wax that helps to keep the outer ear clean.

- The ear canal leads to the eardrum – a thin membrane that separates the outer ear from the middle ear.

- Three 'ossicle' bones are found in the middle ear. These are the malleus (hammer), the incus (anvil) and the stapes (stirrup).

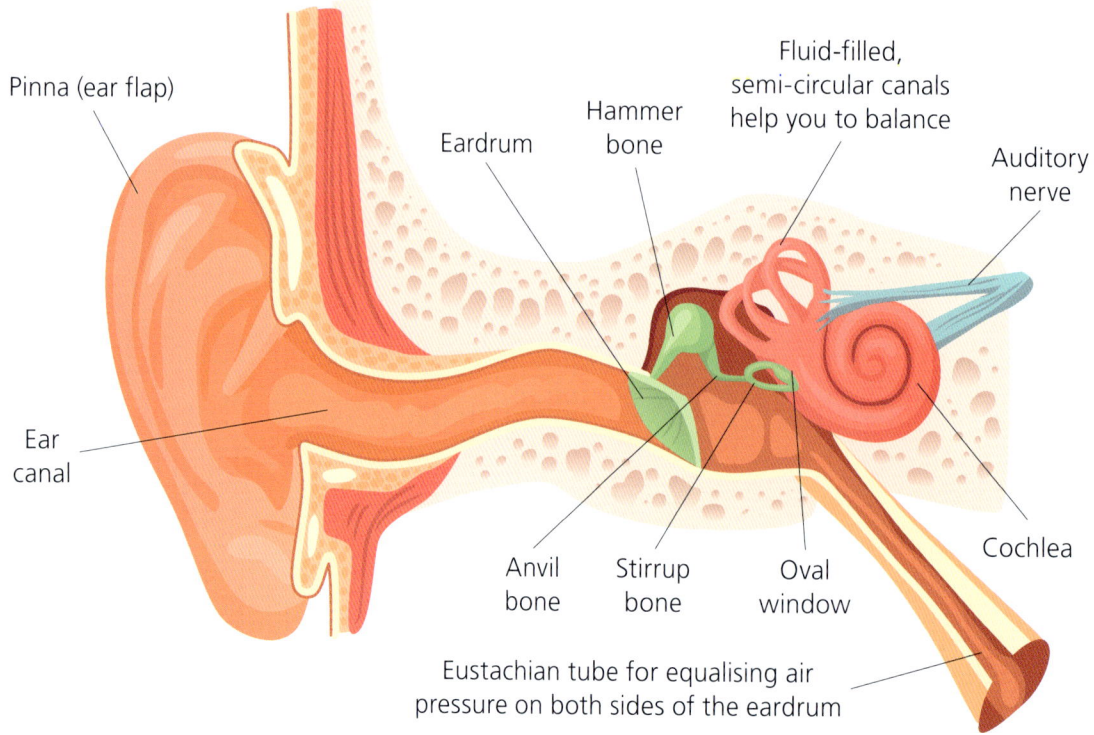

Pinna (ear flap)

Eardrum

Hammer bone

Fluid-filled, semi-circular canals help you to balance

Auditory nerve

Ear canal

Anvil bone

Stirrup bone

Oval window

Cochlea

Eustachian tube for equalising air pressure on both sides of the eardrum

▲ *Most of your ear is hidden inside your head. It is an amazingly complex and delicate structure for picking up the tiny variations in air pressure created by sounds.*

Hearing

👋 Once sounds have travelled down the outer part of your ear, they hit a thin, tight wall of skin – the eardrum – and cause it to vibrate.

👋 When the eardrum vibrates, it shakes the three little bones, known as the ossicles, in the middle ear.

👋 When the ossicles vibrate, they rattle a tiny membrane called the oval window, intensifying the vibration.

👋 The vibration of the oval window makes waves shoot through the liquid in the cochlea, in the inner ear, and wash over the flap of the organ of Corti (above), waving it up and down.

👋 When the organ of Corti waves, it tugs on the many tiny hairs under the flap. These send signals to the brain via the auditory nerve – and you hear a sound.

👋 There are up to 15,000 hair cells in the organ of Corti.

👋 As we get older, we tend to have more difficulty hearing high-pitched sounds. Hearing aids assist people who cannot hear well by amplifying sounds.

👋 Hearing loss can also be the result of being exposed to loud noises over long periods of time, such as regularly listening to music at high volumes.

Organ of Corti

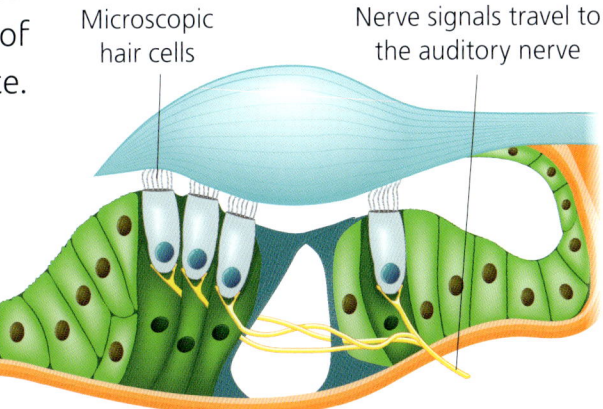

Microscopic hair cells

Nerve signals travel to the auditory nerve

▲ *Vibrations in the fluid in the inner ear are transmitted through nerves, which run through bone to hair cells in the organ of Corti (shown above), which send signals to the brain.*

DID YOU KNOW?
If your hearing is normal, you can hear sounds as deep as 20 hertz (Hz), or 20 vibrations per second, and as high as 20,000 Hz.

Motor nerves

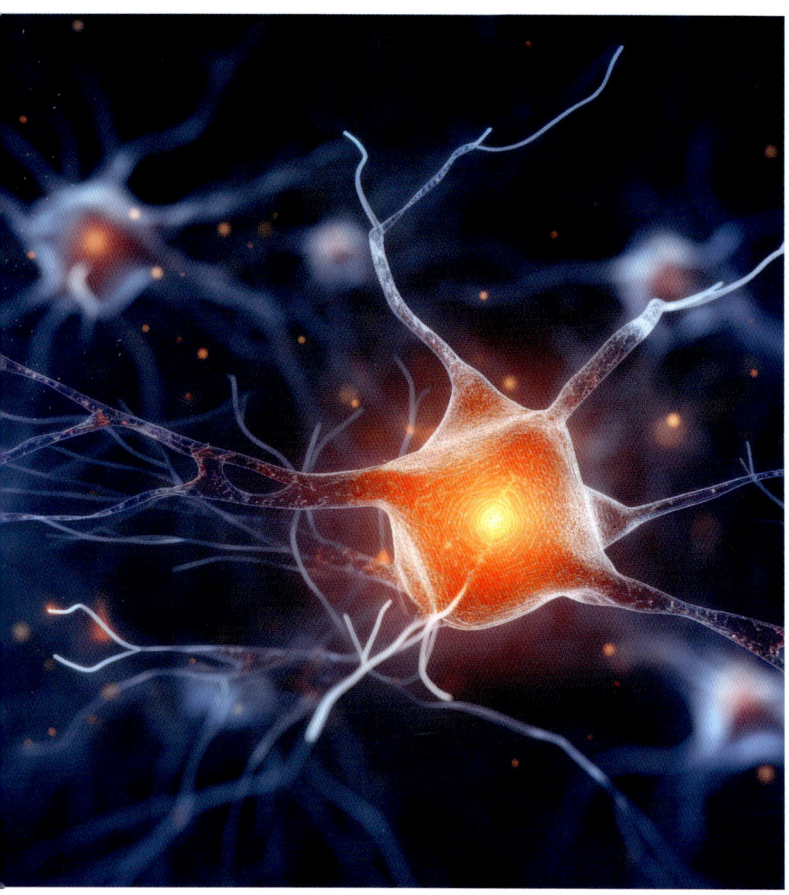

▲ *Signals from the brain – shown here as a flash of orange light – travel down nerve cells to a muscle, commanding the muscle to contract.*

- Motor nerves are connected to your muscles and instruct your muscles to move.

- Each major muscle has many motor nerve endings that tell it to contract (tighten).

- Motor nerves cross over from one side of the body to the other at the top of the spinal cord. This means that signals from the right side of your brain go to the left side of your body, and vice versa.

- Each motor nerve is paired to a 'proprioceptor' on the muscle and its tendons. This sends signals to the brain to say whether the muscle is tensed or relaxed.

- Motor nerve signals come from the brain's motor cortex (see page 48), which works with other parts of the brain to plan and control your voluntary movements.

- The gut has lots of motor nerve endings, but its movements are mostly 'involuntary' – so you feel it but cannot move it consciously.

- The throat has motor nerve endings as well as sensory endings, so you can feel 'protective reflexes' such as coughing and swallowing.

Reflexes

- Reflexes are muscle movements that are automatic – they happen without you even thinking about them.

- Inborn reflexes are reflexes you were born with, such as shivering when you are cold.

- The knee-jerk is an inborn reflex that makes your leg jerk up when the tendon below your knee is tapped.

- Primitive reflexes are reflexes that babies have for a few months after they are born. For example, when you put something into a baby's hand, and it automatically grips it.

- Reflex reactions make you pull your hand from hot things before you have had time to think about it.

- Reflex reactions often 'bypass' the brain. Instead, the alarm signal from your hand sets off motor signals in the spinal cord to move the hand.

- Conditioned reflexes are those you learn through habit, as certain pathways in the nervous system are used again and again.

◄ *Even babies have reflexes – automatically grasping anything put into the palms of their hands.*

Balance

- To stay upright, your body must send a continual stream of data about its position to your brain – and your brain must continually tell your body how to move to maintain its balance.

- Balance is controlled in many parts of the brain, including the cerebellum (see page 47).

- Your brain finds out about your body position from many sources, including your eyes and 'proprioceptors' around the body, as well as the semi-circular canals and other chambers in the inner ear (see page 60).

- Proprioceptors are sense receptors in your skin, muscles and joints.

- The semi-circular canals are three, tiny, fluid-filled loops in your inner ear. Two chambers (spaces) called the utricle and saccule are linked to the semi-circular canals.

- When you move your head, the fluid in the canals and cavities shifts and stimulates cilia, tiny hairs that tell the brain what is going on.

- The canals tell you whether you are nodding or shaking your head, and which way you are moving.

- The utricle and saccule tell you if you are tilting your head, or if its movement is speeding up or slowing down.

◄ *This gymnast's body is feeding her brain a stream of data about its position to help her stay balanced.*

Coordination

▼ *The eyes follow the ball to tell the brain exactly where it is. The brain also relies on a high-speed stream of sensory signals from the proprioceptor cells in order to tell it exactly where the leg is, and to keep the body balanced.*

DID YOU KNOW?
Proprioceptors allow you to touch the exact tip of your nose, even with your eyes shut.

- Coordination is the process of organising balance or skilful movement.

- To make you move, your brain has to send signals out along nerves, which tell all the muscles involved exactly what to do.

- Coordination of the muscles is handled by the cerebellum at the back of your brain (see page 47).

- The cerebellum is given instructions by the brain's motor cortex. Its own commands are then sent via the basal ganglia in the middle of the brain.

- Proprioceptors are nerve cells that are sensitive to movement, pressure or stretching. Proprioceptor basically means 'one's own sensors'.

- They are all over the body, from the tiny hair cells in the balance organs of the ear to the muscles, tendons and joints. Each one sends signals to the brain, giving it the position or posture of every part of your body.

Thinking

- Some scientists claim that we humans are the only living things that are conscious, meaning that we alone are actually aware that we are thinking.

- No one knows how consciousness works – it is one of science's last great mysteries.

- Most of your thoughts seem to take place in the cerebrum (at the top of your brain), and different kinds of thought are linked to different areas, known as association areas.

- Each half of the cerebrum has four rounded ends, called lobes.

- The two lobes at the front are known as the frontal and temporal lobes, and the two at the back are called the occipital and parietal lobes.

- The frontal lobe is linked to your personality and it is where you have your bright ideas.

- The temporal lobe is where you hear and understand what people are saying to you.

- The occipital lobe is where you work out what your eyes see.

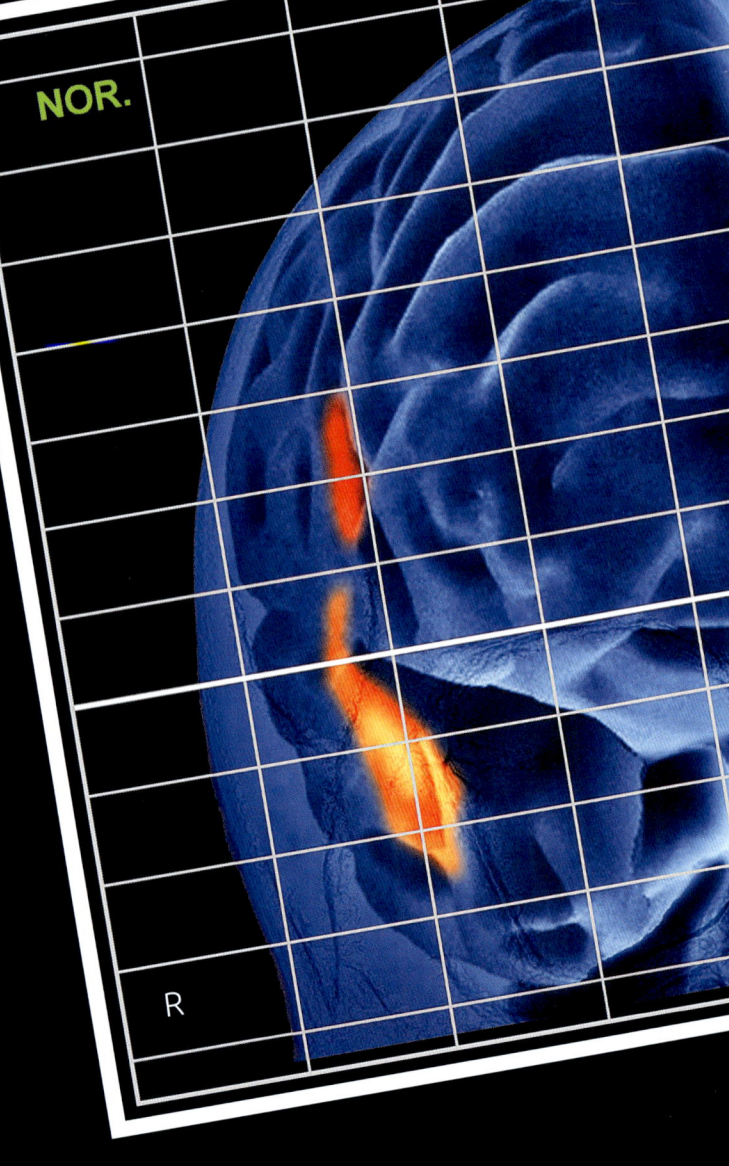

NOR.

R

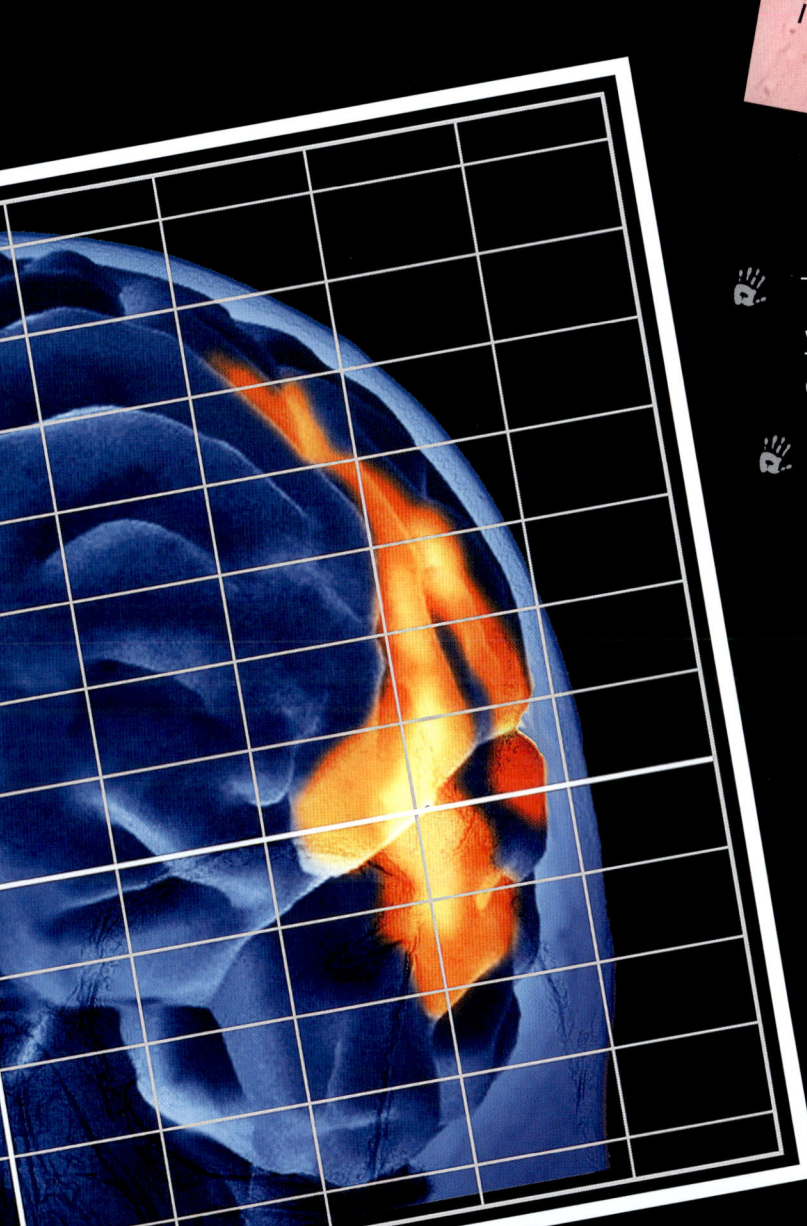

The parietal lobe is where you register touch, heat and cold, and pain.

The left half of the brain (left hemisphere) controls the right side of the body. Meanwhile, the right half (right hemisphere) controls the left side.

One half of the brain is always dominant (in charge). Usually, the left brain is dominant, which is why up to 90 per cent of people in the world are right-handed.

Mood

▶ *Changes in the body can alter the way you feel – the act of smiling can make you feel more positive.*

DID YOU KNOW?
Every mood is a combination of how much energy you have and how stressed you are.

🖐 Your state of mind is your mood – whether you are happy or sad, angry or afraid, overjoyed or irritable.

🖐 Emotions and moods seem to be strongly linked to the structures in the centre of the brain, where unconscious activities are controlled.

🖐 Moods have three elements – how you feel, what happens to your body, and what moods make you do.

🖐 Certain memories or experiences are so strongly linked in your mind that they can often trigger a certain mood automatically.

🖐 Symptoms of a low mood may include feeling sad, anxious or panicky, angry or frustrated, more tired – or unable to sleep.

🖐 A low mood often gets better after a few days or weeks. It is possible to improve a low mood by making small changes, such as getting more sleep, more exercise, or by talking to someone about how you feel.

🖐 Scientists are only just beginning to discover how moods and emotions are linked to particular parts of the brain.

Memory

- When you commit something to memory, your brain probably stores it by creating new nerve connections.

- You have three types of memory – sensory, short-term and long-term.

- Sensory memory is when you go on feeling a sensation for a moment after it has stopped.

- Short-term memory is when the brain stores things for a few seconds, such as a phone number you remember long enough to press the correct buttons on the handset.

- Long-term memory is memory that can last for months or maybe even your whole life.

DID YOU KNOW?
Your short-term memory can store only about four or five things at once.

HOW TO IMPROVE YOUR MEMORY	
CHUNKING	To remember a long string of numbers, for example, break it down into smaller chunks
SPACING IT OUT	Don't cram – space out your learning rather than trying to remember everything at once
CUES	Use something you do or say every day to help you remember other things
IMAGERY	Visualising images as you are learning can help you to recall items or names
SELF-REFERENCE	It is easier to remember something if you can link it with something personal
PLACE THINGS	To remember a collection of things, try imagining them in specific places in your home or somewhere familiar

Communication

We communicate in many different ways, not just through spoken words but also through our tone of voice, facial expressions and our body language.

Although we are the only animals to use a complicated spoken and written language, all animals use sounds and body language in their communication.

We use our vocal cords to speak, and we interpret other people's speech using the brain. However, it is not just what we say that is important: the brain also interprets the tone and 'nuance' (shades of meaning) in people's voices to help us understand what is meant.

Your facial expression, posture and pose all contribute to your body language, which is thought to provide up to 70 per cent of all human communication.

ASL SIGN LANGUAGE

▲ In its simplest form, sign language can spell out any word using hands alone. Hundreds of different sign languages are used around the world.

▲ *People at a sports event reveal their excitement through their body language.*

Body language can reveal whether you are telling the truth. In a game of poker, card players may deliberately use their expressions and body language to mislead or 'bluff' their opponents.

Body language can also reveal whether you are bored, confident, anxious – or interested in someone.

It is often easy to tell someone's mood just by looking at their face. You have more than 40 muscles in your face – all of which can be used to create a huge variety of facial expressions.

Sign language is an important form of communication for people who cannot hear. A combination of hand, body and facial gestures is used to express words and phrases.

Sign language is not just for deaf people: divers use it to communicate with each other underwater, while soldiers use it for passing on vital instructions at times when silence is needed to maintain safety.

The hypothalamus

The hypothalamus is a tiny area of the brain that controls the glands in the body and our metabolism (the conversion of food and drink into energy).

It helps to regulate your sleep, hunger, thirst, blood pressure, your body's temperature and fluid balance.

Nerve signals are constantly being sent to and from the hypothalamus to make sure the body's temperature, blood pressure and heart rate are all correct.

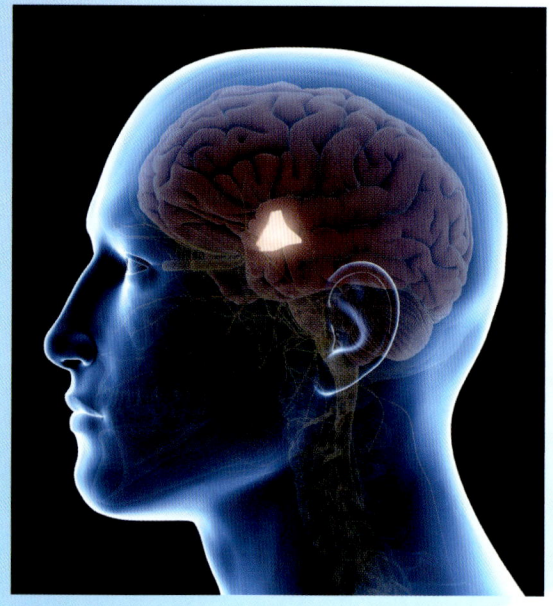

▲ *The hypothalamus is a complex area of the brain that has a number of important responsibilities.*

- The hypothalamus also gives out hormones – known as releasing hormones – that act on the pituitary gland.

- These releasing hormones encourage the pituitary gland to give out the hormones that affect growth and reproduction.

- The hypothalamus controls the circadian cycle – your internal 'body clock'.

- Your body clock is set to a 24-hour cycle. Stimulated by daylight, it tells us when we should be alert, eating and sleeping.

- People who fly across the world to a very different time zone experience a 'jet lag'. Their internal body clock is still set to the 'local time' back at home – and so their body rhythms are disrupted.

- The hypothalamus also controls hunger and thirst.

DID YOU KNOW?
The word circadian comes from the Latin words 'circa', meaning 'around', and 'diem', meaning 'day'.

◄ When people travel across time zones they get 'jet lag'. It often takes a few days for their internal body clock to adjust to the new time zone.

Sleeping

- When you are asleep, many of your body functions go on as normal, and your brain goes on receiving sense signals. Meanwhile, your body has a chance to save energy and carry out routine repairs.

- Lack of sleep can be dangerous. A newborn baby needs 18–20 hours of sleep each day. An adult needs around seven to eight hours.

- Sleep is controlled in the brain stem. Dreaming is stimulated by signals fired from a part of the brain stem called the pons.

- When you are awake, there is little pattern to the electricity created by the firing of the brain's nerve cells. However, as you sleep, more regular waves appear.

- While you are asleep, alpha waves sweep across the brain every 0.1 seconds. Theta waves arrive in early sleep and are less frequent.

- For the first 90 minutes of sleep, your sleep gets deeper and the brain waves become stronger (as theta waves are replaced by delta waves).

▼ *As we grow, we require less sleep. Toddlers and young children need around 11–15 hours of sleep per day.*

STAGE 1
Light sleep and can
be easily awakened

STAGE 2
Eye movement
and brain waves
slowing down

STAGE 3
Delta waves begin
to appear

STAGE 4
Deep sleep, difficult
to wake up

STAGE 5
Breathing
becomes more
rapid and
irregular

◀ *There are said
to be five main
stages of sleep.*

After about 90 minutes of sleep, your brain suddenly starts to buzz with activity, yet you are hard to wake up.

After that first 90 minutes, your eyes begin to flicker from side to side beneath their lids. This is known as Rapid Eye Movement (REM) sleep.

REM sleep is thought to show that you are dreaming.

During a full sequence of sleep, your ordinary 'deeper' sleep state alternates with spells of REM sleep that get progressively longer, eventually lasting around an hour.

DID YOU KNOW?
You sleep is greatly influenced by your body's internal clock – the circadian cycle.

Temperature

The inside of your body stays at a constant temperature of around 37°C (98°F), rising a few degrees only when you are ill.

Your body creates heat through its metabolism – complex chemical reactions in the cells that transfer the energy in food into energy for the body, such as the 'energy sugar' glucose.

Even at rest, your body generates so much heat that you are comfortable only when the air is slightly cooler than you are.

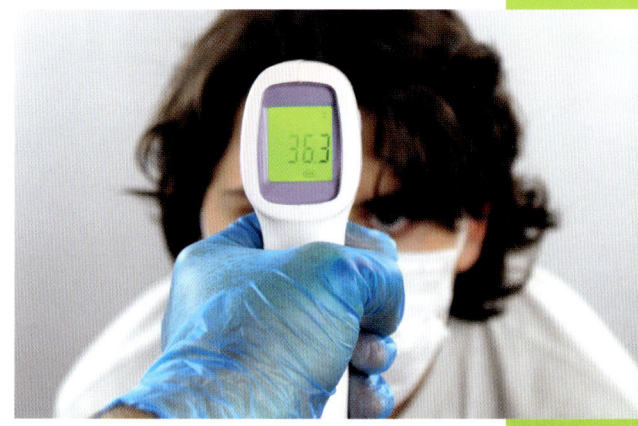

▲ The body's temperature can be easily monitored using a digital thermometer.

When you are working hard, your muscles can create as much heat as a 2-kilowatt electric room heater.

Your body loses heat as you breathe in cool air and breathe out warm air. Your body also loses heat by giving it off from your skin.

The tiny hypothalamus, located in the middle of the brain, is your body's temperature control.

Temperature sensors in the skin, in the body's core, and in the blood tell the hypothalamus how hot or cold your body is.

If the body is too hot, the hypothalamus sends signals to your skin telling it to sweat more. Signals also tell blood vessels in the skin to widen, allowing heat to escape from the blood as it nears the skin's surface.

If the body is too cold, the hypothalamus commands the skin to narrow its blood vessels and restrict blood flow there. It also emits signals to tell the muscles to generate more heat by making the body shiver.

The hypothalamus may also stimulate the thyroid gland to send out hormones to make your cells burn energy faster – thus generating more heat when the body needs it.

▶ *This thermal image shows how, on a hot day, the skin becomes flushed as blood vessels widen to try to lose heat. Drinking something cold can help to cool the body.*

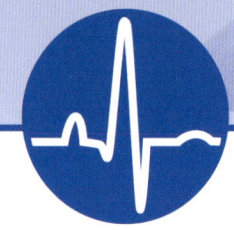

Circulation

Your circulation is the system of tubes, or blood vessels, that carries blood out from your heart to all of your body cells – and back again.

The body's tissues receive fresh blood continuously, although the blood flow is delivered in rhythmic pulses.

On the way out from the heart, blood is pumped through vessels called arteries and arterioles.

On the way back to the heart, blood flows through venules and veins.

Blood flows from the arterioles to the venules through the very tiniest vessels – the capillaries.

Blood circulation has two parts: the pulmonary and the systemic.

▲ *During exercise, the heart rate increases to circulate the blood more quickly, getting extra oxygen and nutrients to your muscles.*

The pulmonary circulation carries oxygen-poor blood from the right side of the heart to the lungs for 'refuelling'. It then returns oxygen-rich blood to the left side of the heart.

The systemic circulation carries oxygen-rich blood from the left side of the heart all around the body. It returns blood that is low in oxygen to the right side of the heart.

Oxygen is carried by haemoglobin, a protein found in red blood cells.

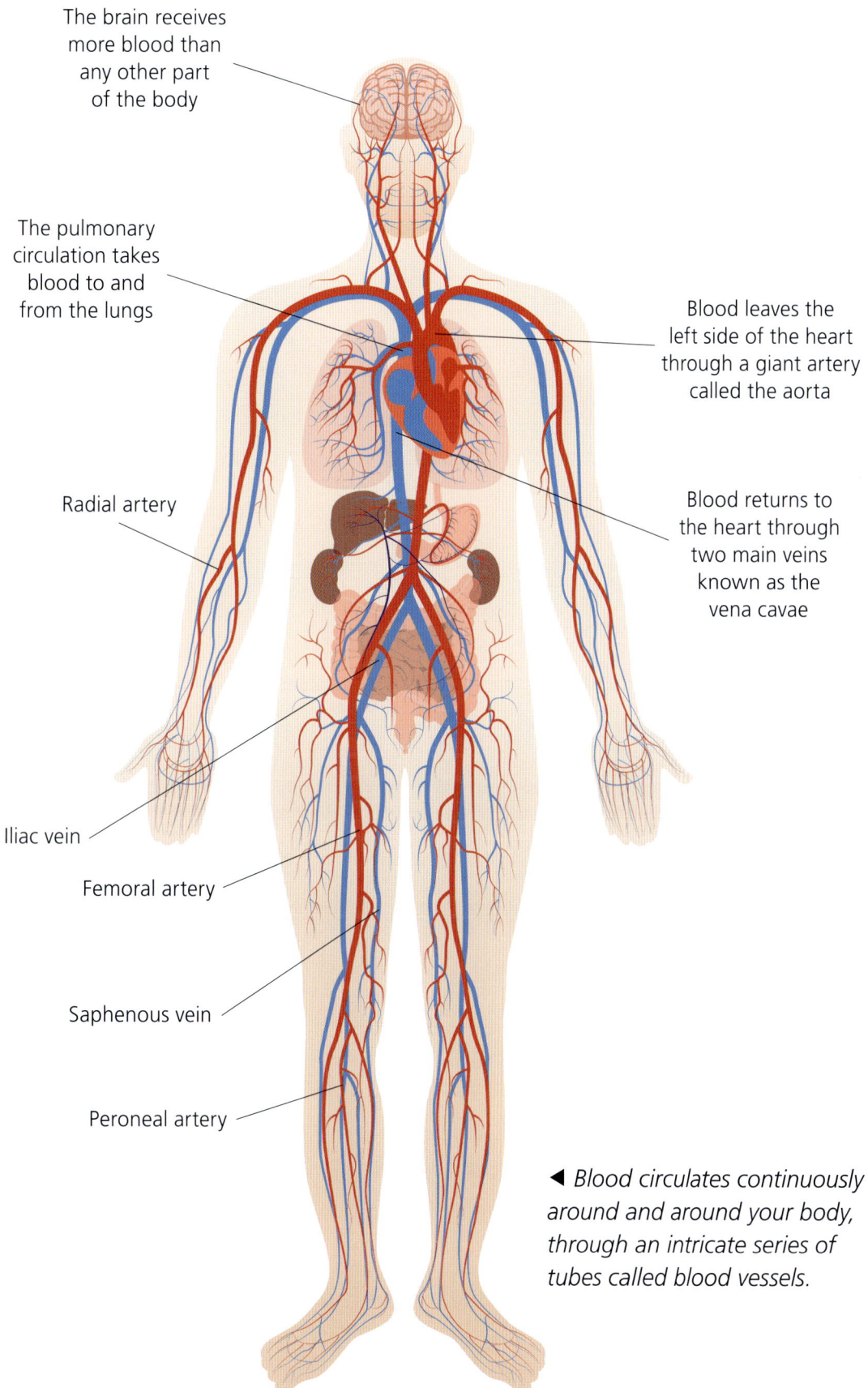

The brain receives more blood than any other part of the body

The pulmonary circulation takes blood to and from the lungs

Blood leaves the left side of the heart through a giant artery called the aorta

Radial artery

Blood returns to the heart through two main veins known as the vena cavae

Iliac vein

Femoral artery

Saphenous vein

Peroneal artery

◀ *Blood circulates continuously around and around your body, through an intricate series of tubes called blood vessels.*

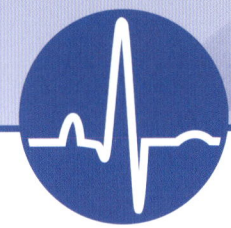

The heart

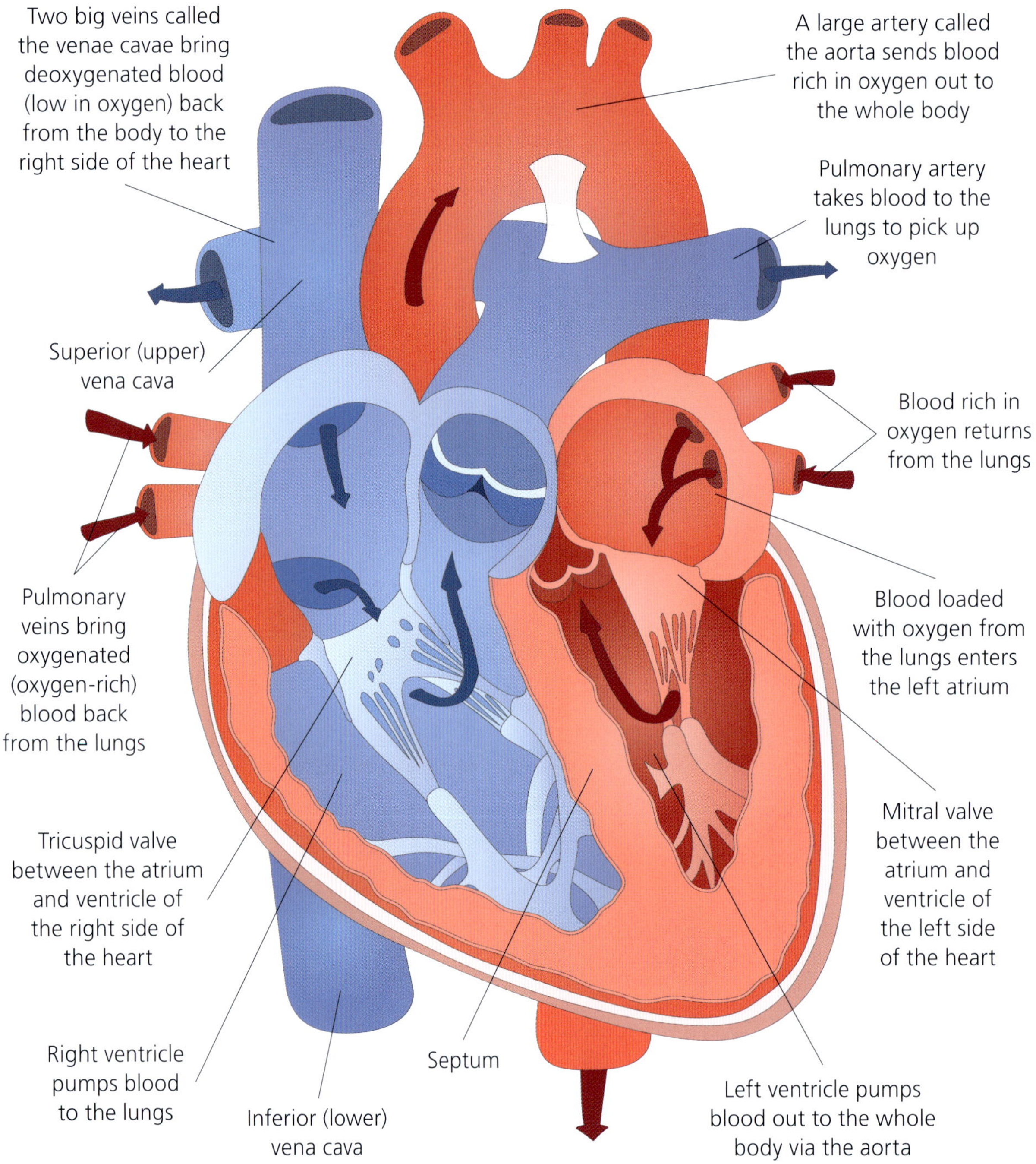

Two big veins called the venae cavae bring deoxygenated blood (low in oxygen) back from the body to the right side of the heart

A large artery called the aorta sends blood rich in oxygen out to the whole body

Pulmonary artery takes blood to the lungs to pick up oxygen

Superior (upper) vena cava

Blood rich in oxygen returns from the lungs

Pulmonary veins bring oxygenated (oxygen-rich) blood back from the lungs

Blood loaded with oxygen from the lungs enters the left atrium

Tricuspid valve between the atrium and ventricle of the right side of the heart

Mitral valve between the atrium and ventricle of the left side of the heart

Right ventricle pumps blood to the lungs

Septum

Inferior (lower) vena cava

Left ventricle pumps blood out to the whole body via the aorta

▲ *The heart is a remarkable 'double pump', with two pumping chambers – the left ventricle and the right ventricle. It contracts automatically to squeeze jets of blood out of the ventricles and through the arteries.*

- Your heart is roughly the size of your fist. It is located in the centre of your chest, slightly to the left.

- The heart is a powerful pump made almost entirely of muscle.

- The heart contracts (tightens) and relaxes automatically about 70 times a minute to pump blood out through your arteries.

- The heart has two sides separated by a muscle wall called the septum.

- The right side is smaller and weaker, and it pumps blood only to the lungs.

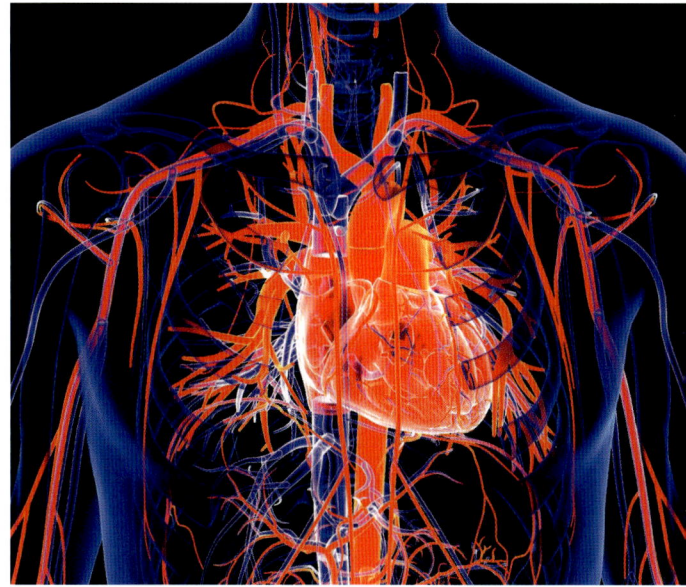

▲ *During an average lifetime, the heart pumps approximately 200 million litres of blood.*

- The stronger left side pumps blood all around the body.

- Each side of the heart has two chambers. There is an atrium (plural: atria) at the top of each chamber, where blood delivered by the veins accumulates (builds up). Below each atrium is a ventricle that contracts to pump blood out into the arteries.

- The ventricles have much thicker, muscular walls and are much stronger than the atria. This is because they are needed to pump blood a lot further around the body.

- Each side of the heart (left and right) ejects about 70 millilitres (ml) of blood with every heartbeat.

- The coronary arteries supply the heart. If they become clogged, the heart muscle may become short of blood and stop working. This is what happens during a heart attack.

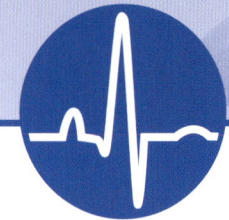

Heart valves

There are two valves in each side of the heart to make sure the blood flows in one direction only.

When the ventricles contract, the blood in the chamber pushes back against the flaps of the valves, closing them and preventing blood from flowing back into the atria.

The aortic valve guards the exit from the left ventricle into the aorta.

The pulmonary valve guards the exit from the right ventricle, which leads into the pulmonary artery.

Heart valves are put under a lot of stress and strain and may become damaged or diseased. Occasionally, a valve may not form properly and not work correctly from birth.

Damaged valves can be replaced by artificial ones, or with organic valves from human donors or pigs.

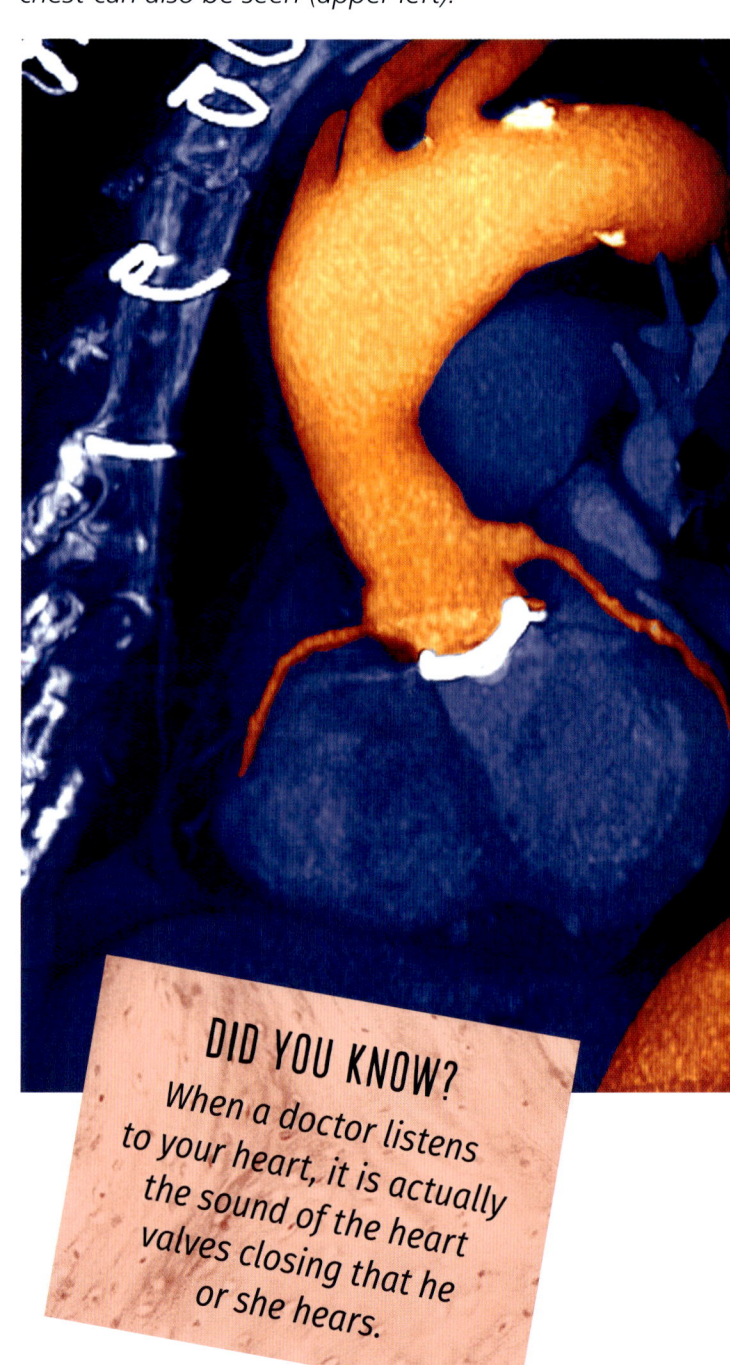

▼ This coloured scan shows an artificial heart valve (white, at the centre) where the main artery in the body, the aorta, enters the heart. The stitches used to close the chest can also be seen (upper left).

DID YOU KNOW?
When a doctor listens to your heart, it is actually the sound of the heart valves closing that he or she hears.

Heartbeat

Right atrium   Left atrium   Valves open

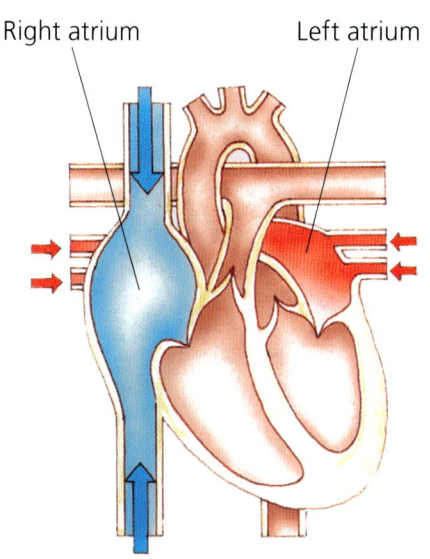
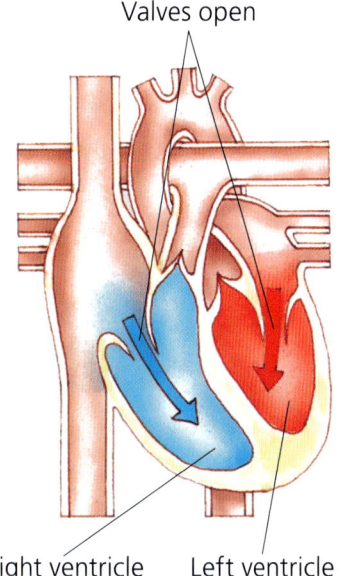
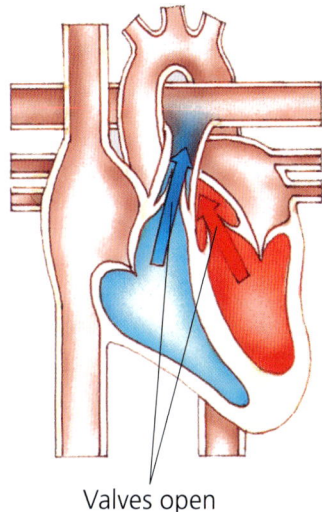

Right ventricle   Left ventricle   Valves open

1 *Blood floods into the relaxed atria.*

2 *The wave of contraction squeezes blood into the ventricles below.*

3 *Blood is squeezed out of the ventricles into the arteries.*

- The heartbeat is the regular squeezing of the heart muscle to pump blood around the body.

- It is also the term given to the 'lub-dup' sound that the heart makes when it beats, which can be heard through a stethoscope.

- The heartbeat sequence is called the cardiac cycle and it has two phases – systole and diastole. Systole is when the heart muscle contracts (tightens). Diastole is the resting phase between the heart's contractions.

Blue: deoxygenated blood to the lungs   Red: oxygenated blood to body

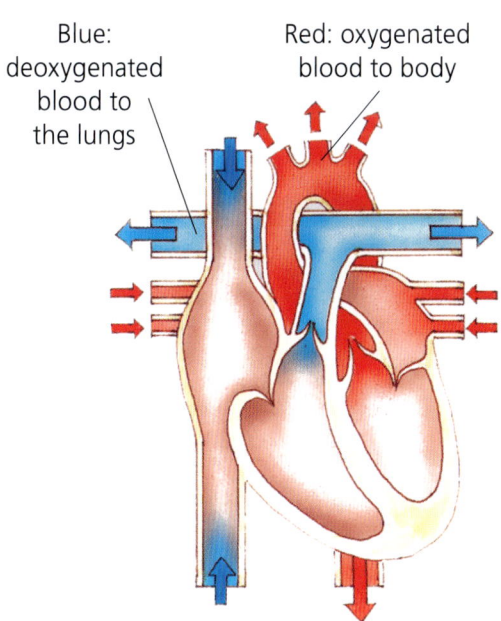

4 *Blood starts to fill up the now-relaxed atria again.*

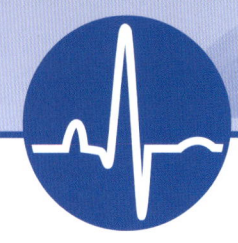

Pulse

- Your pulse is the powerful, high-pressure surge that runs through your blood as the heart contracts strongly with each beat.

- You can feel your pulse by placing two fingertips on the inside of your wrist where the radial artery (see page 79) nears the surface.

- Other pulse points include the carotid artery in the neck and the brachial artery inside the elbow.

- Normal pulse rates vary between 50 and 100 beats per minute (BPM). The average for a man is about 71 BPM; for a woman it is 80 BPM; and for children it is approximately 85 BPM.

- Tachycardia is the medical term for an abnormally fast heart rate, while bradycardia is an abnormally slow heart rate.

- An 'arrhythmia' refers to any abnormality in a person's heart rate.

- Anyone with a heart problem may be connected to a machine called an electrocardiogram (ECG) to monitor (observe) their heartbeat.

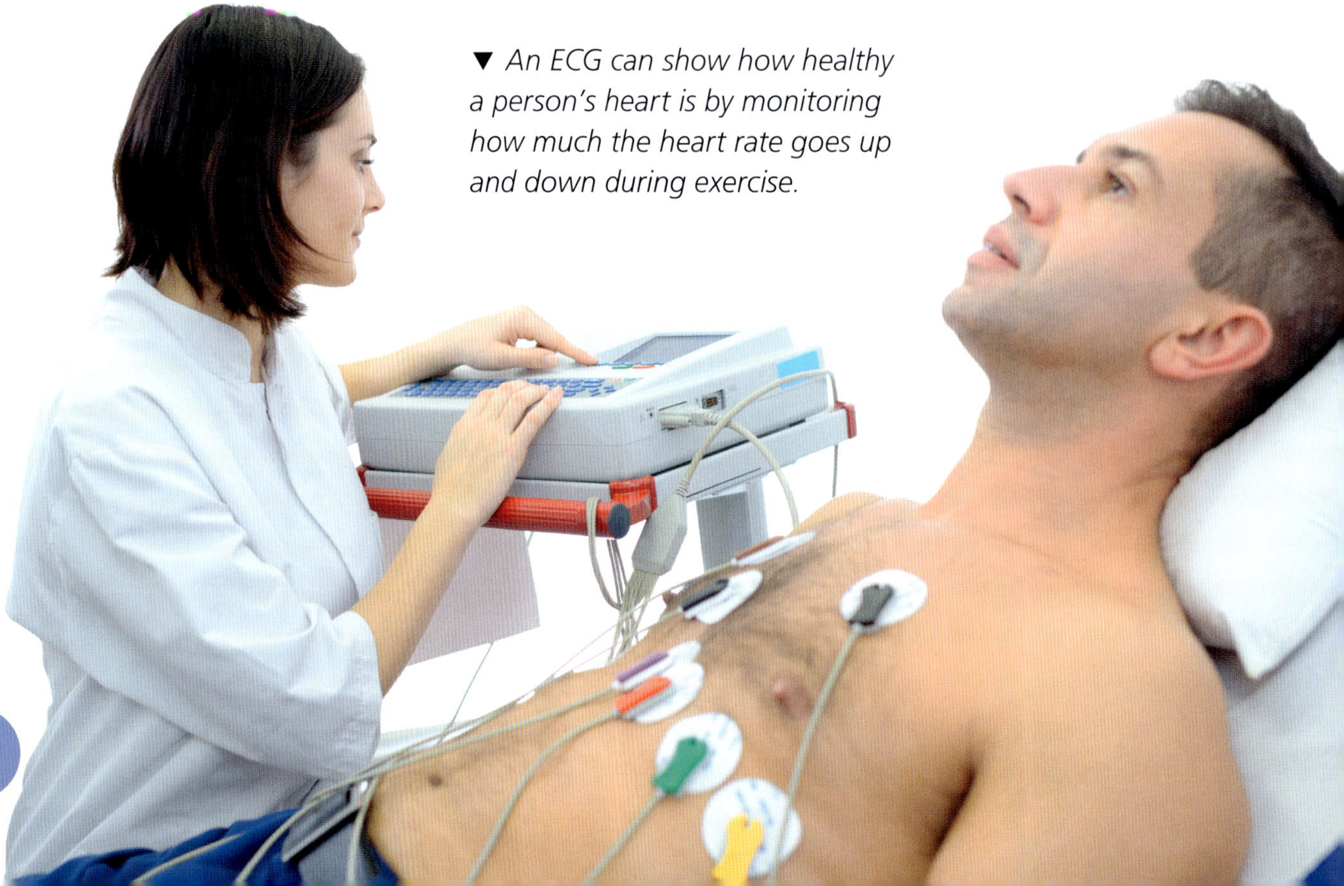

▼ *An ECG can show how healthy a person's heart is by monitoring how much the heart rate goes up and down during exercise.*

Arteries

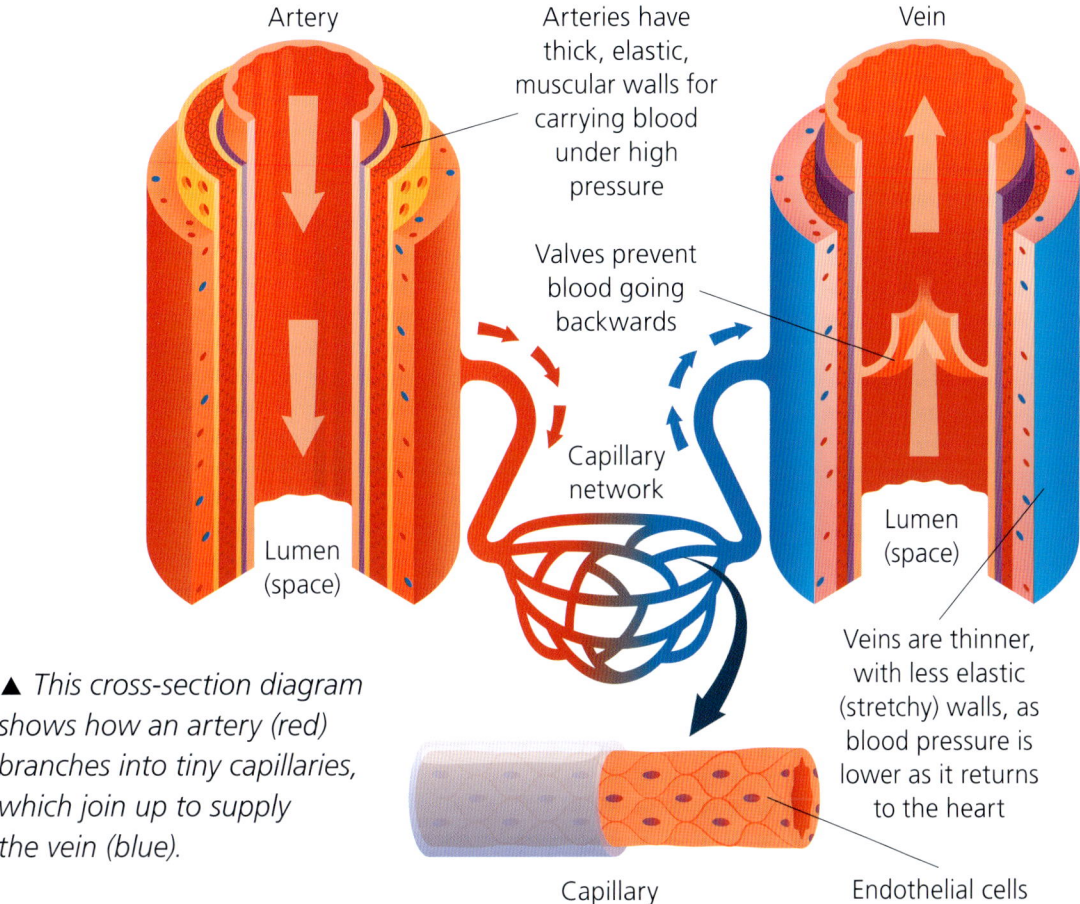

Artery

Arteries have thick, elastic, muscular walls for carrying blood under high pressure

Vein

Valves prevent blood going backwards

Capillary network

Lumen (space)

Lumen (space)

Veins are thinner, with less elastic (stretchy) walls, as blood pressure is lower as it returns to the heart

Capillary

Endothelial cells

▲ *This cross-section diagram shows how an artery (red) branches into tiny capillaries, which join up to supply the vein (blue).*

Arteries are normally the vessels that carry blood away from the heart.

An arteriole is a smaller vessel that branches off from an artery. Arterioles branch into microscopic capillaries.

Blood flows through arteries at 30 cm per second in the main artery, down to 2 cm or less per second in the smaller arterioles.

Arteries run alongside most of the veins that return blood to the heart.

The walls of arteries are muscular and can expand or relax to control the rate at which the blood is flowing.

Arteries have thicker, stronger walls than veins – and the pressure created by the blood inside them is a lot higher.

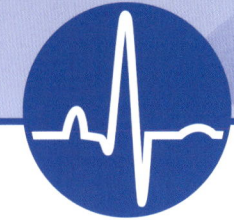

Veins

KEY VEINS
1 Jugular vein
2 Brachial vein
3 Pulmonary vein
4 Vena cava

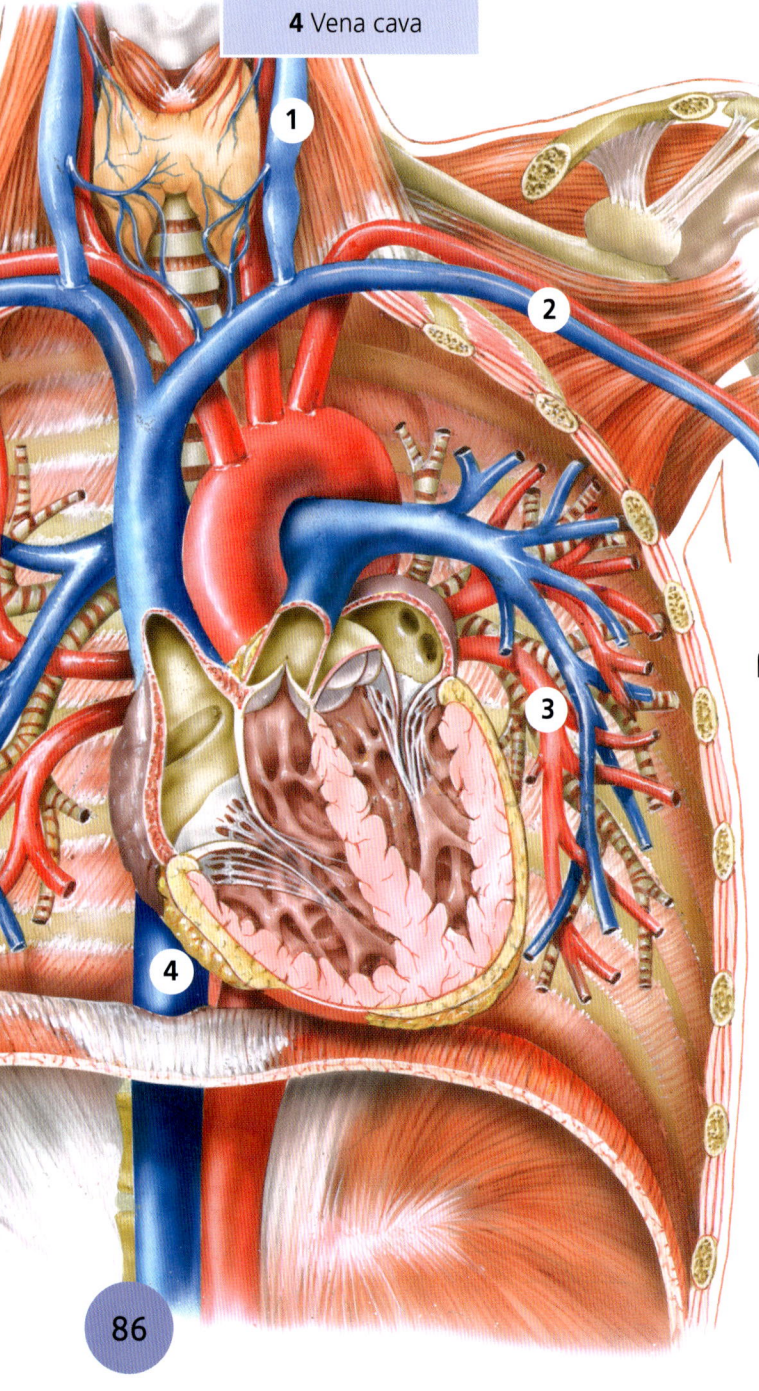

Veins are small tubes, or vessels, in the body designed to carry blood back to the heart.

Most veins carry 'used' blood back to the heart, once the body cells have taken the oxygen they need from the blood.

When blood is low in oxygen, it is a dark, purplish-blue colour, unlike the bright red of the 'oxygenated' blood carried by the arteries.

The only veins that carry oxygenated blood are the four pulmonary veins, which carry blood from the lungs to the heart.

The two largest veins in the body are the vena cavae, which flow directly into the heart.

Most veins have flaps that act as valves, which ensure that the blood flows in one direction only.

DID YOU KNOW?
At any one moment, 70–75 per cent of the body's blood is in the veins.

◄ *Most veins carry blood back to the heart.*

Capillaries

- Capillaries are the smallest of all your blood vessels, visible only under a microscope. They link the arterioles to the venules.

- There are more than ten billion capillaries in the human body.

- The largest capillary is just 0.2 mm wide – thinner than a human hair.

- Each capillary is approximately 0.5 mm to 1 mm in length.

- Capillary walls are just one cell thick, which makes it easy for chemicals to pass through them.

- It is through the capillary walls that your blood passes oxygen, food nutrients and waste to and from your body cells.

- Capillaries carry more blood towards the skin's surface when you are warm (see page 76). They carry less to keep blood away from the skin's surface (and save heat) when you are cold.

DID YOU KNOW?
The average capillary is 0.001 mm in diameter – just wide enough for red blood cells to pass through it, one at a time.

► You generate heat when exercising, which the body tries to lose by opening up capillaries in the skin, making it appear red.

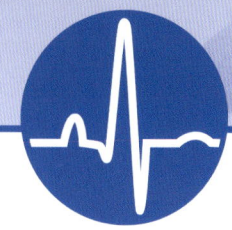

Blood

- Blood is the reddish liquid that circulates around your body. It carries oxygen and nutrients (from food) to body cells, and takes carbon dioxide and other waste products away. It fights infection, keeps you warm, and distributes chemicals that control body processes.

- Blood is made up of red cells, white cells and platelets, all carried in a liquid called plasma.

- Plasma is 90 per cent water, plus hundreds of other substances, including nutrients, hormones and special proteins designed to fight infection.

- Blood plasma turns milky immediately after a meal high in fats.

- Platelets are tiny pieces of cell that clump together to form blood clots at the site of a wound – to stop bleeding.

DID YOU KNOW?
Oxygen in the air turns blood bright red when you bleed. In your veins it can be almost brown in colour.

◀ *Blood contains millions of cells, carried in a clear, straw-coloured liquid called plasma.*

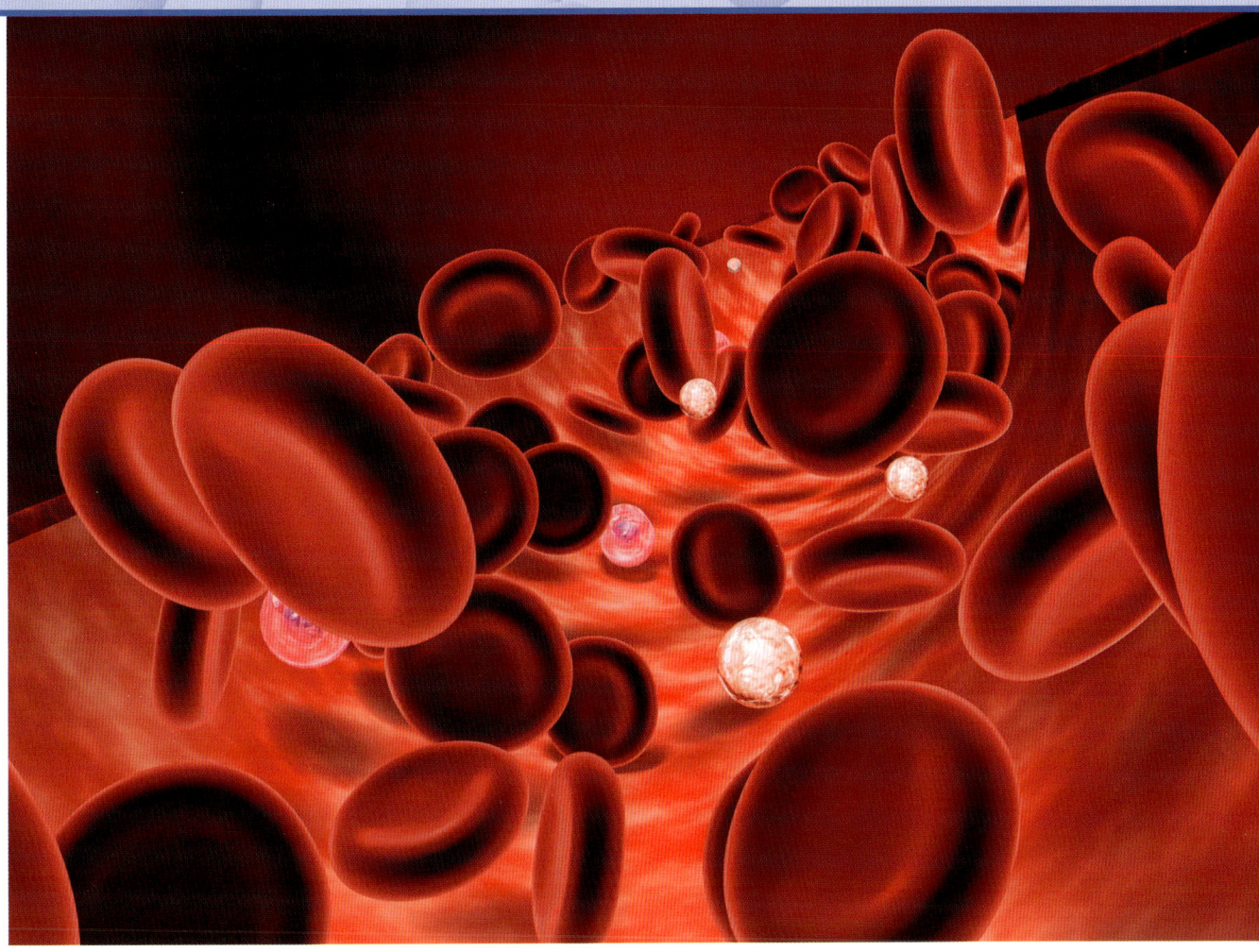

▲ *Oxygen is carried in the blood by red blood cells,*
attached to a special protein called haemoglobin.

The amount of blood in your body depends on your size. An adult who weighs 80 kg has about 5 litres of blood. A child who is half as heavy has around half as much blood.

If a blood donor gives 0.5 litres of blood, the body replaces the plasma in a few hours – but it takes a few weeks to replace the red blood cells.

It takes about one minute for your blood to circulate around your body. If you are exercising and your heart is beating rapidly, blood can circulate all the way round your body in about 20 seconds.

A drop of blood the same size as the dot on this 'i' contains around five million red cells.

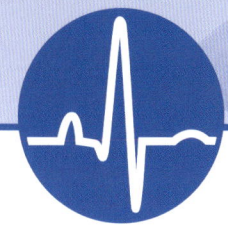

Blood cells

- Your blood has two main kinds of cell – red cells and white cells – plus pieces of cell called platelets.

- Red blood cells are button-shaped and they contain a red protein called haemoglobin, which contains iron.

- Haemoglobin is a substance that enables the red blood cells to ferry oxygen around your body.

- Red cells also contain enzymes, which the body uses to make certain chemical processes happen.

- White blood cells are big cells, also known as leucocytes. Most types of white cells are involved in fighting infections.

- Most white cells are granulocytes, which contain tiny little granules.

- The majority of granulocytes are giant white cells called neutrophils. These are the blood's cleaners – their task is to eat up invaders.

▼ *Button-shaped red blood cells carry oxygen through the blood. Spiky, ball-shaped white blood cells help your body to fight infection.*

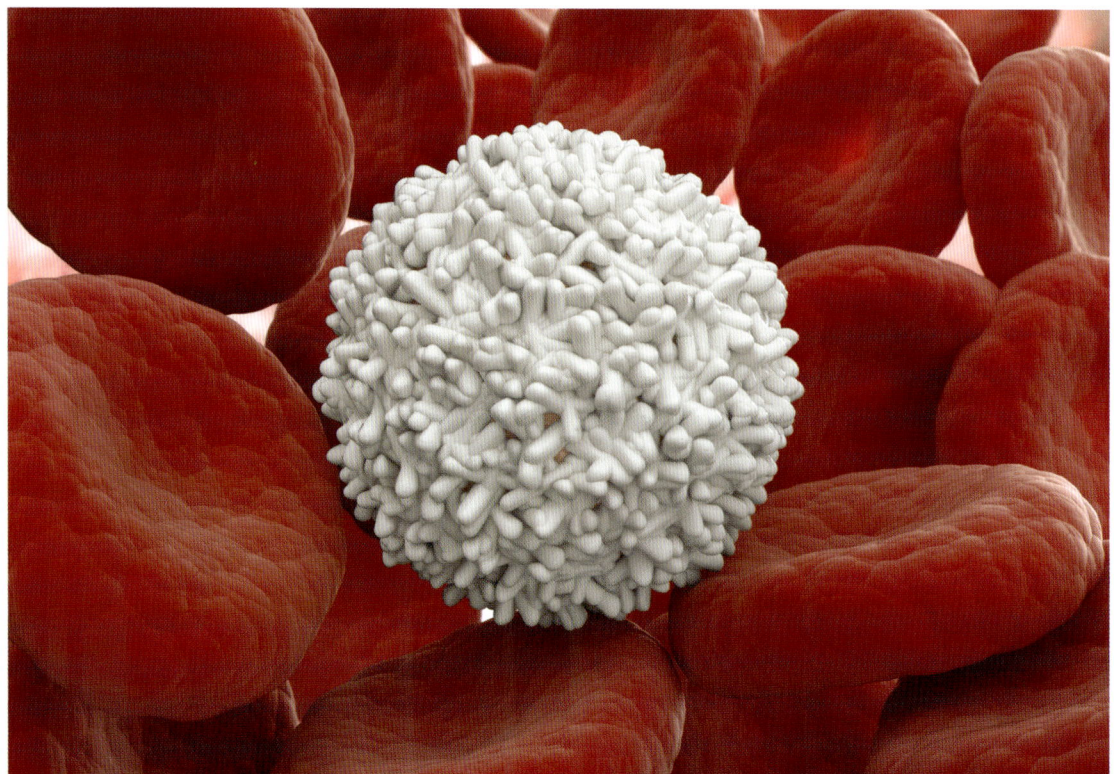

Bone marrow

- Marrow is the soft, jellylike tissue in the middle of certain bones.

- Bone marrow is either red (if it is rich in blood tissue) or yellow (rich in fat tissue).

- Red bone marrow is the body's blood factory. This is where all blood cells, apart from some white cells, are created.

- All the different kinds of blood cell start life in red marrow as one type of cell called a stem cell. Different blood cells then develop as the stem cells divide and re-divide.

- Some stem cells divide to form red blood cells and platelets.

- Other stem cells divide to form lymphoblasts. In turn, these divide to form various different types of white cells, such as monocytes and lymphocytes.

- The white cells made in bone marrow play a key part in the body's immune system. This is why bone-marrow transplants can help people with illnesses that affect their immune system.

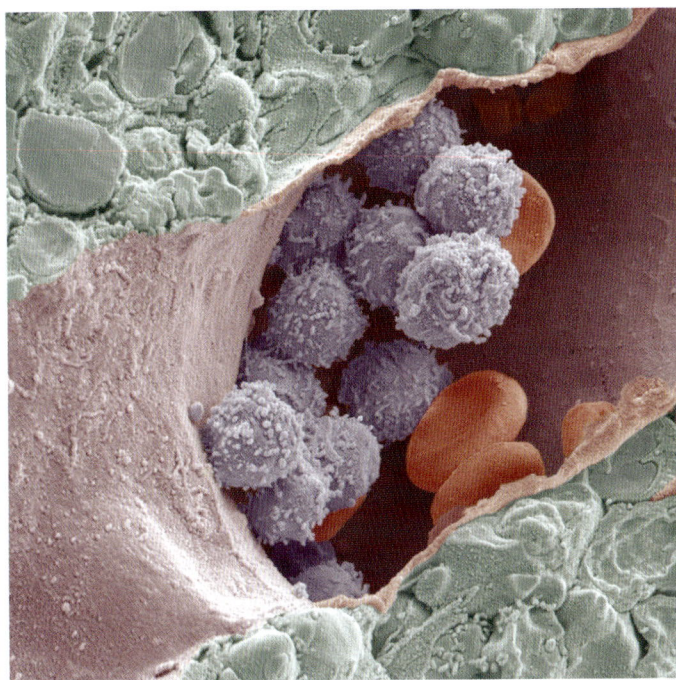

▲ *Inside most bones is a core called marrow. In some bones, there is red marrow (shown here in green), where most blood cells are made.*

▼ *Some varieties of blood cell are shown below.*

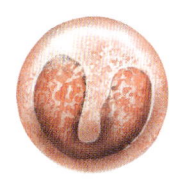

RED BLOOD CELL

EOSINOPHIL

BASOPHIL

PLATELETS

NEUTROPHIL

MONOCYTE

LYMPHOCYTE

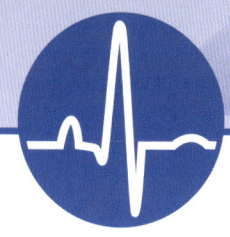

Blood groups

- Most people's blood belongs to one of four different groups or types – A, O, B and AB.

- Blood type O is the most common, followed by blood group A.

- Blood is also either Rhesus positive (Rh+) or Rhesus negative (Rh-).

- Approximately 85 per cent of people are Rh+.

- If your blood is Rh+ and your group is A, your blood group will be 'A positive'. If your blood is Rh- and your group is O, you are 'O negative'.

- A transfusion involves giving blood to a patient from another person's body. The patient's blood type is 'matched' with stored or donated blood considered safe for transfusion.

- Blood transfusions are given when someone has lost too much blood due to an injury or operation. They are also given to replace diseased blood.

▼ *Blood donors usually donate about 500 ml of blood at a time and are able to donate every two months or so.*

DID YOU KNOW?
'O negative' blood donors are called universal donors, because their blood can be given without causing a bad reaction in the recipient.

Wound healing

- When we injure ourselves, a series of chemical reactions follows.

- White blood cells appear at the scene of the wound to fight infection.

- Platelets begin to stick to each other – and to the walls of the damaged blood vessels.

- The sticky platelets attract more platelets, forming a 'plug' to stop you losing too much blood.

- The platelets release a sequence of chemicals called clotting factors (factors 1 through to 8).

- At the final stage of the clotting sequence, a lacy, fibrous network is formed from a protein called fibrin.

- The fibrin traps red blood cells to form a blood clot that seals the damaged vessel.

- The damaged vessel slowly repairs itself and the clot then gradually dissolves. Any clots on the surface of the skin turn into scabs, which gradually dry up and fall off.

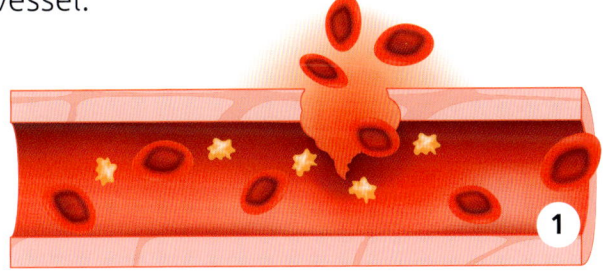

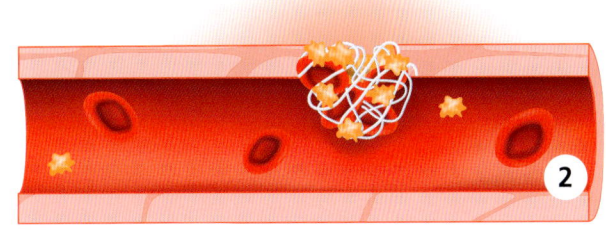

▶ When you are injured, red blood cells **(1)** and platelets **(2)** leak out into the surrounding tissues, and a sticky substance called fibrin **(3)** is produced to help heal the wound.

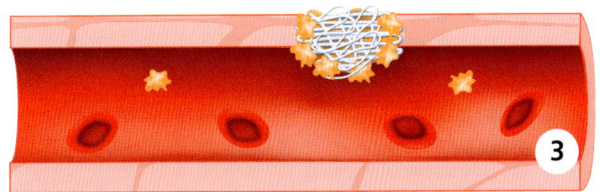

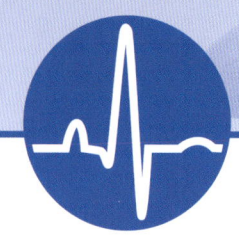

Respiratory system

- The respiratory system consists of the airways and the lungs.

- The system performs gas exchange – exchanging oxygen (in the air that we breathe in) for carbon dioxide (in the air that we breathe out).

- As air is inhaled (drawn in), it passes through the nose, down the airways and into the lungs. Air being exhaled (breathed out) passes in the opposite direction.

- The respiratory system works in partnership with the circulatory system to make sure that every cell in the body receives oxygen and is able to get rid of its waste carbon dioxide.

- The respiratory system takes up most of the space in the chest.

- The lungs and the lower part of the airways are enclosed and protected by the ribs.

- Muscles in the rib cage contract and relax as we inhale and exhale.

- A large, dome-shaped muscle underneath the lungs, called the diaphragm, also contracts and relaxes as we breathe in and out.

DID YOU KNOW?
If you could open up your lungs and lay them out flat, they would cover half a football field.

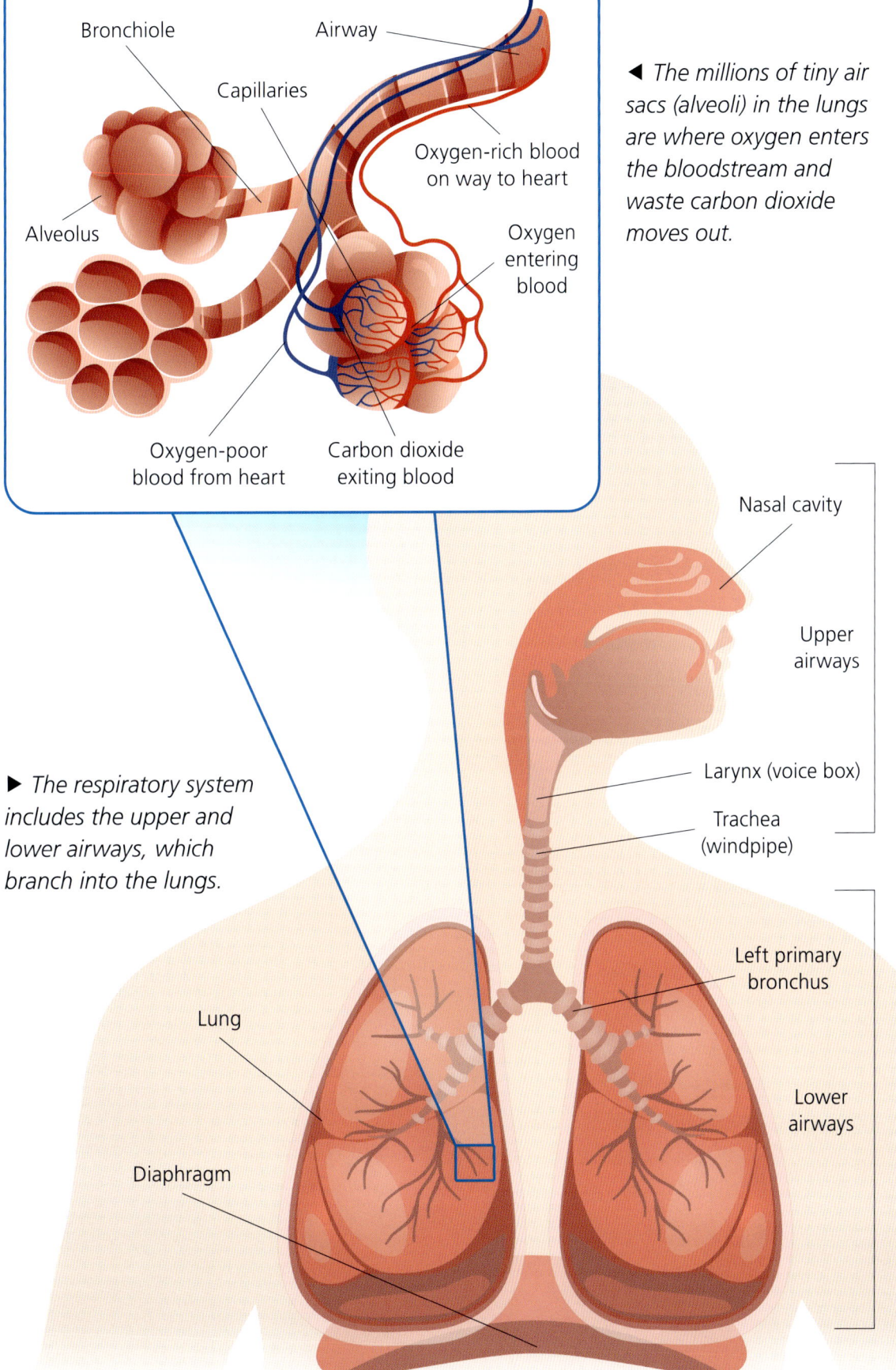

Bronchiole

Airway

Capillaries

Oxygen-rich blood
on way to heart

Alveolus

Oxygen
entering
blood

Oxygen-poor
blood from heart

Carbon dioxide
exiting blood

◄ *The millions of tiny air
sacs (alveoli) in the lungs
are where oxygen enters
the bloodstream and
waste carbon dioxide
moves out.*

Nasal cavity

Upper
airways

Larynx (voice box)

Trachea
(windpipe)

► *The respiratory system
includes the upper and
lower airways, which
branch into the lungs.*

Left primary
bronchus

Lung

Lower
airways

Diaphragm

95

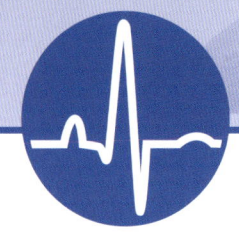

The lungs

- Your lungs are a pair of soft, spongy bags inside your chest.

- The lungs consist of bunches of minute air sacs called alveoli.

- Bunches of alveoli are found at the ends of bronchioles, small airways that eventually connect to larger airways and to the throat.

- Alveoli are surrounded by a network of tiny blood vessels. Alveoli walls are just one cell thick – thin enough to allow oxygen and carbon dioxide to seep through them. The walls have a large enough surface area to enable huge quantities to seep in and out of the blood.

- There are more than 300 million alveoli in your lungs.

- It is possible to survive with just one lung, if one becomes damaged.

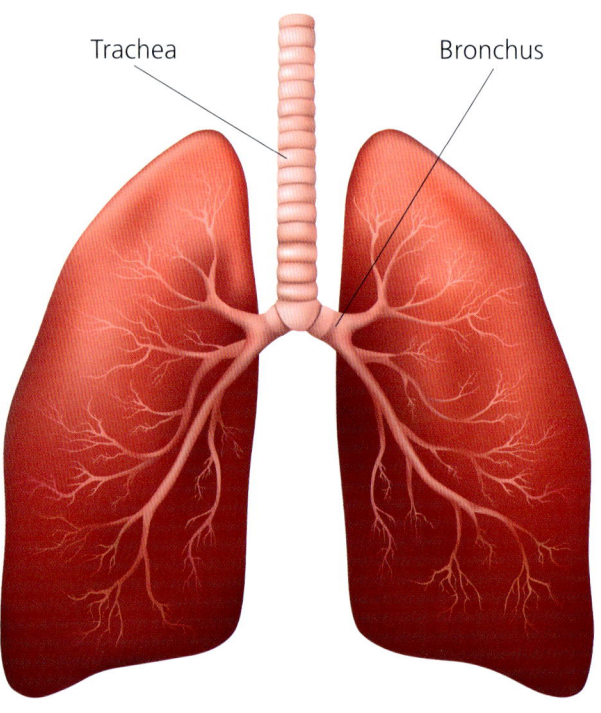

Trachea

Bronchus

▲ *Your trachea divides into two tubes called bronchi. One enters each lung.*

▶ *Taken through a powerful microscope, this photo of a slice of lung tissue shows a blood vessel and the very thin walls of an alveolus next to it.*

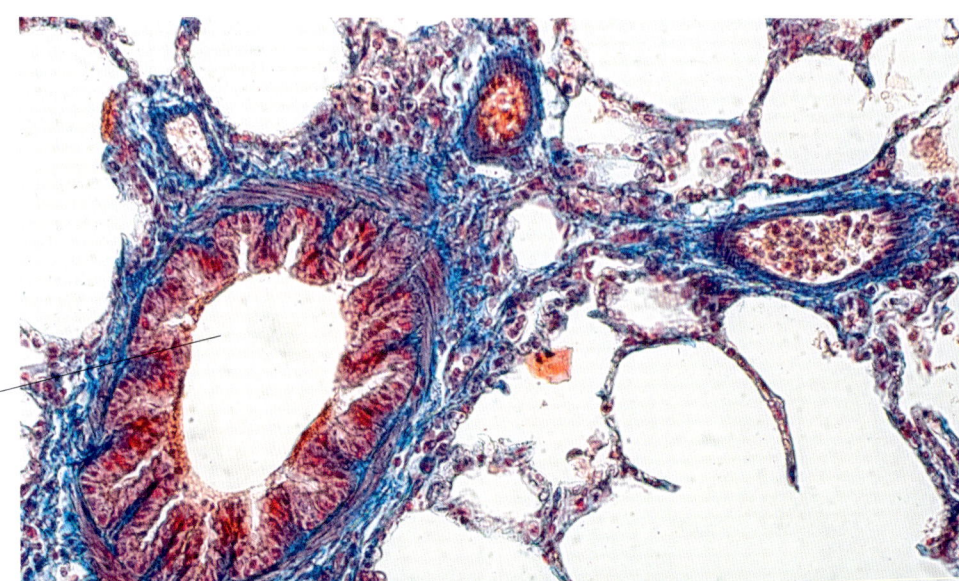

Blood vessel

Breathing

- You respire (breathe) because every single cell in your body needs a continuous supply of oxygen to 'burn' or break down glucose, the high-energy substance from digested food that cells receive from the blood.

- Scientists call breathing 'respiration'. Cellular respiration is the process by which cells use oxygen to break down glucose.

- When you inhale, air rushes in through your nose or mouth, down your windpipe and into the millions of branching airways in your lungs.

- On average, you breathe in about 15 times every minute. If you run energetically, the rate soars to around 80 times a minute.

- A normal breath takes in about 0.4 litres of air. A deep breath can take in around ten times as much.

- Your diaphragm is a dome-shaped sheet of muscle between the chest and stomach, which works in partnership with your chest muscles.

- Breathing is automatic and controlled by the brain. However, we can consciously make ourselves breathe faster or hold our breath.

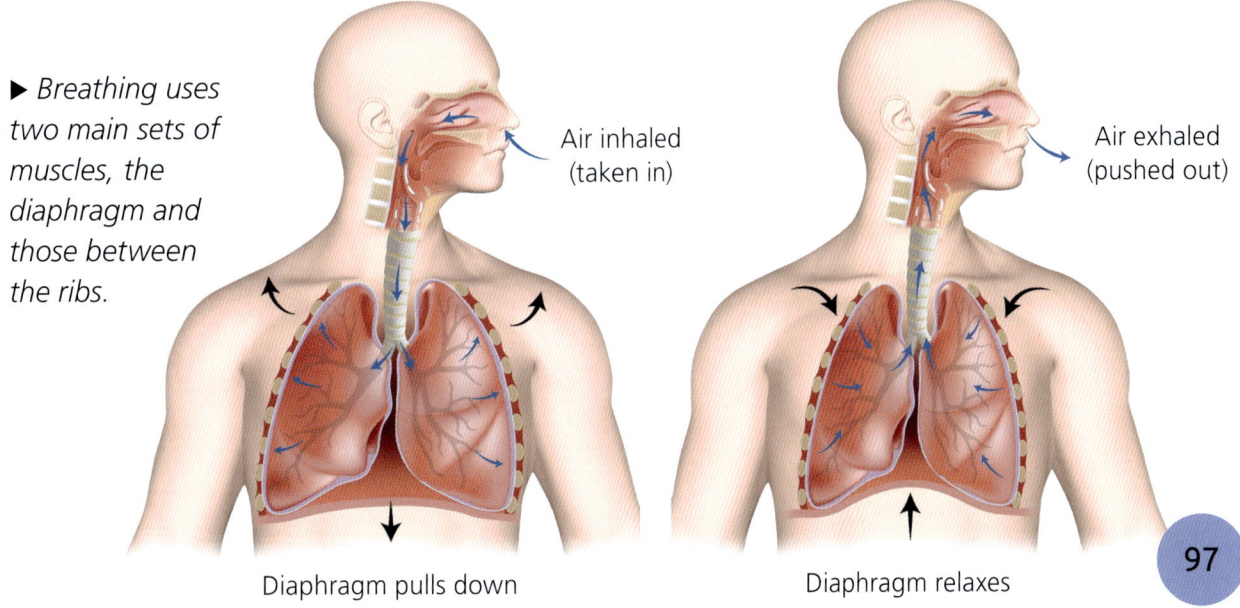

▶ Breathing uses two main sets of muscles, the diaphragm and those between the ribs.

Air inhaled (taken in)

Air exhaled (pushed out)

Diaphragm pulls down

Diaphragm relaxes

Digestion

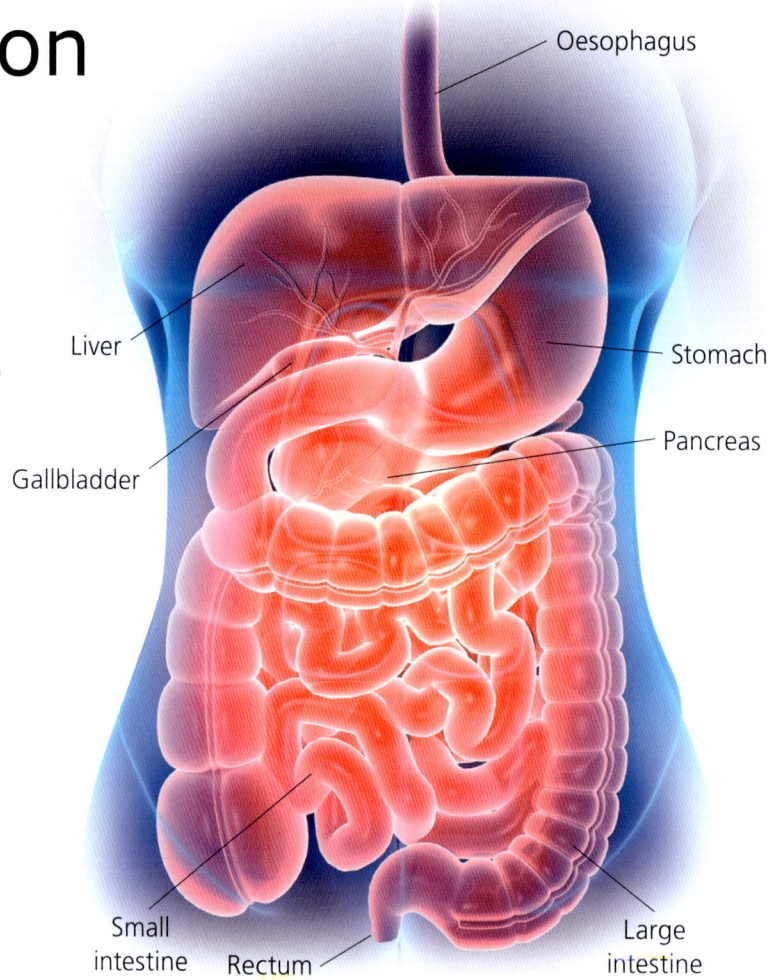

Oesophagus

Liver

Stomach

Gallbladder

Pancreas

Small intestine

Rectum

Large intestine

▲ *Food is passed to the stomach through the oesophagus. Once it has been processed by the stomach, it progresses to the small intestine.*

- Digestion is the process by which your body breaks down the food you eat into substances that it can absorb (take in) and use.

- Your food is partly broken down by mechanical processes, such as chewing and movements in the gut, and partly by chemical enzymes.

- The food you eat is softened in your mouth by chewing and by chemicals in your saliva (spit).

- When you swallow, food travels down your oesophagus (gullet) and into your stomach.

- The stomach partly digests the food, turning it into a thick liquid called chyme. Gradually, chyme is released into the small intestine.

- The chyme is broken down even more inside the small intestine. It is then absorbed through the wall of the gut and into the blood.

- Food that cannot be absorbed in the small intestine passes on into your large intestine. It is then pushed out through the anus as faeces when you go to the toilet.

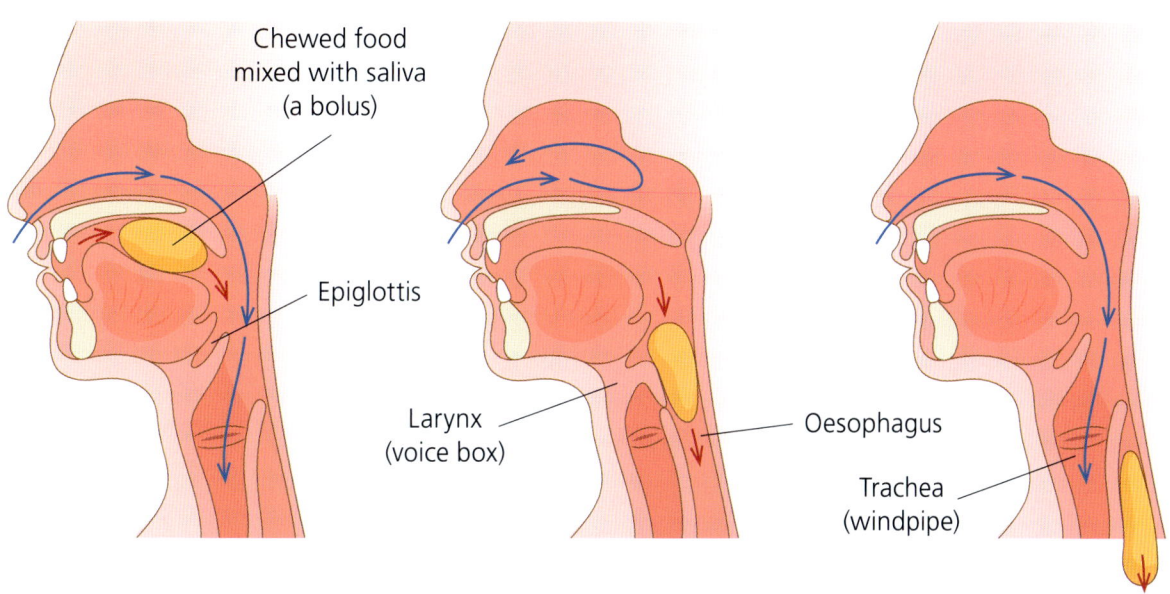

1   **2**   **3**

Chewed food mixed with saliva (a bolus)

Epiglottis

Larynx (voice box)

Oesophagus

Trachea (windpipe)

▲ *After chewing (1), food is swallowed into the oesophagus (2). Waves of muscular contractions – known as peristalsis – push the food down through the chest (3), past the heart and lungs, and into the stomach.*

- Digestion begins as soon as food enters the mouth: enzymes start working on it, while chewing breaks the food up and softens it.

- As we chew, the salivary glands around the mouth produce saliva that helps to soften the food, making it much easier to swallow.

- Enzymes in the saliva also begin to break down and digest the food.

- The soft palate, a flap of tissue at the back of the mouth, is pressed upwards to stop food from getting into your nose.

- The epiglottis, a flap of cartilage at the top of the windpipe, tilts down over the larynx to prevent food from entering the airways.

- The swallowed food passes the closed-off airways and enters the top of the digestive tract – the oesophagus.

- Wave-like, muscular movements in the oesophagus squeeze and push the food towards its next destination – the stomach.

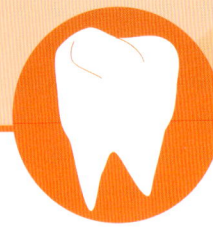

Enzymes

- Enzymes are molecules that are almost always proteins, and which alter the speed of chemical reactions in living things.

- There are thousands of enzymes inside your body – it would not be able to function properly without them.

- Some enzymes need an extra substance, called a coenzyme, in order to work. Many coenzymes are vitamins.

- The 'messenger RNAs' are one of the most important enzyme groups. They are used as communicators by the nuclei of body cells.

- Many enzymes are essential for the digestion of food, including lipase, protease, amylase, and the peptidases. Many of these enzymes are manufactured in the pancreas.

- Lipase, an enzyme that helps to break down fats, is produced mainly by the pancreas and is released into the alimentary canal (or gut).

- Amylase breaks down starches, such as those in bread and fruit, into simple sugars. There is amylase in saliva and in the stomach.

◄ *Saliva contains enzymes called amylase and lipase that begin to break down food as soon as it enters your mouth.*

The stomach

- Your stomach is a bag with muscular walls that mashes food into a pulp, assisted by chemicals called gastric juices.

- When empty, your stomach holds barely 0.5 litres, but after a big meal it can stretch to contain more than 4 litres.

- The sight, smell and taste of food all stimulate the production of gastric juices, so that the stomach is ready to perform its job by the time the food reaches it.

- The gastric juices produced by the stomach contain acid and enzymes designed to break down proteins.

- The stomach takes up to five hours to mix and digest solid food.

- Once the food has been reduced to thick, semi-liquid chyme (see page 98), a muscular ring at the stomach's exit relaxes, and the chyme enters the small intestine.

▶ *The strong muscles of the stomach enable it to churn food, while the folded lining allows it to expand.*

DID YOU KNOW?
The stomach lining is protected by mucus to stop it from digesting itself.

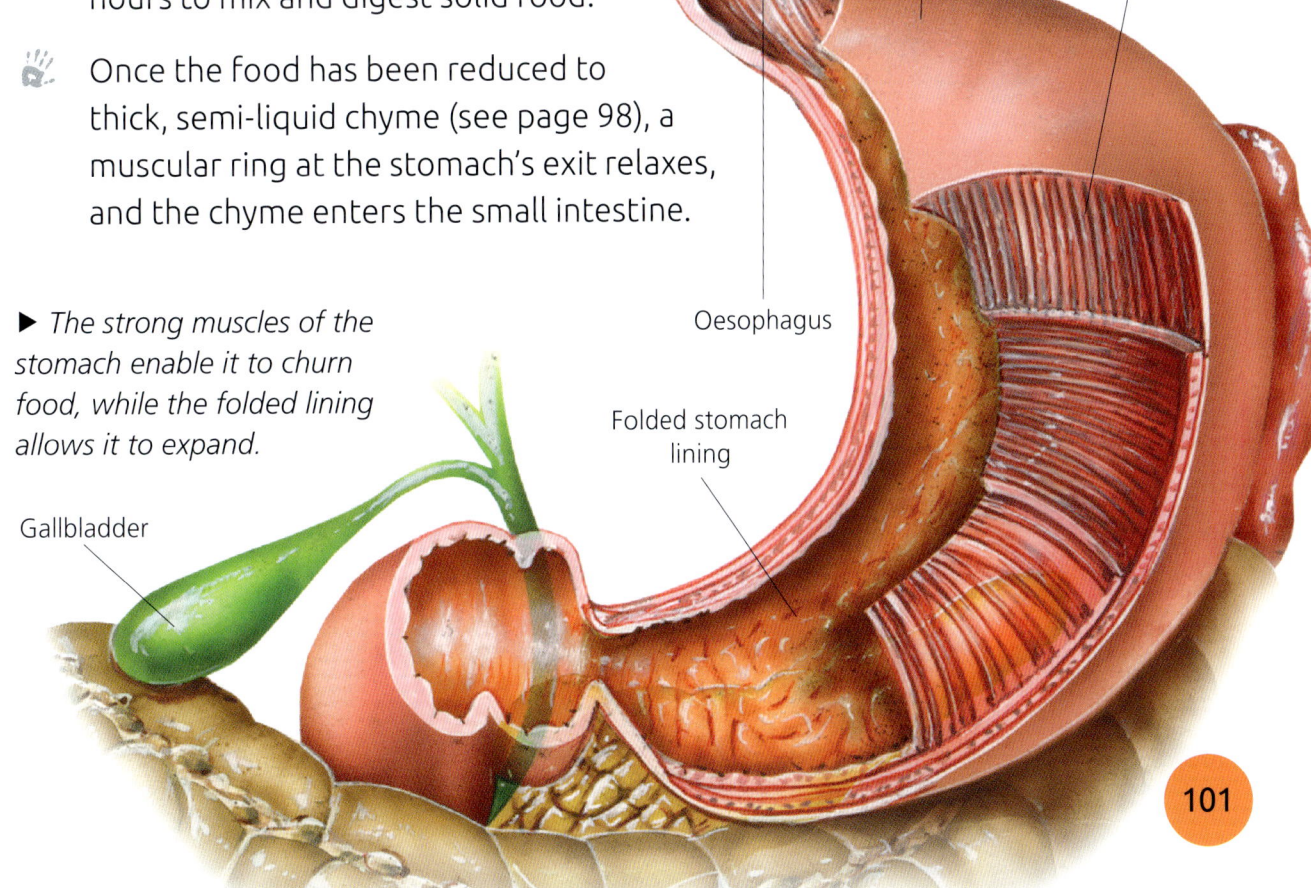

Outer wall of stomach

Muscular layers

Oesophagus

Folded stomach lining

Gallbladder

The liver

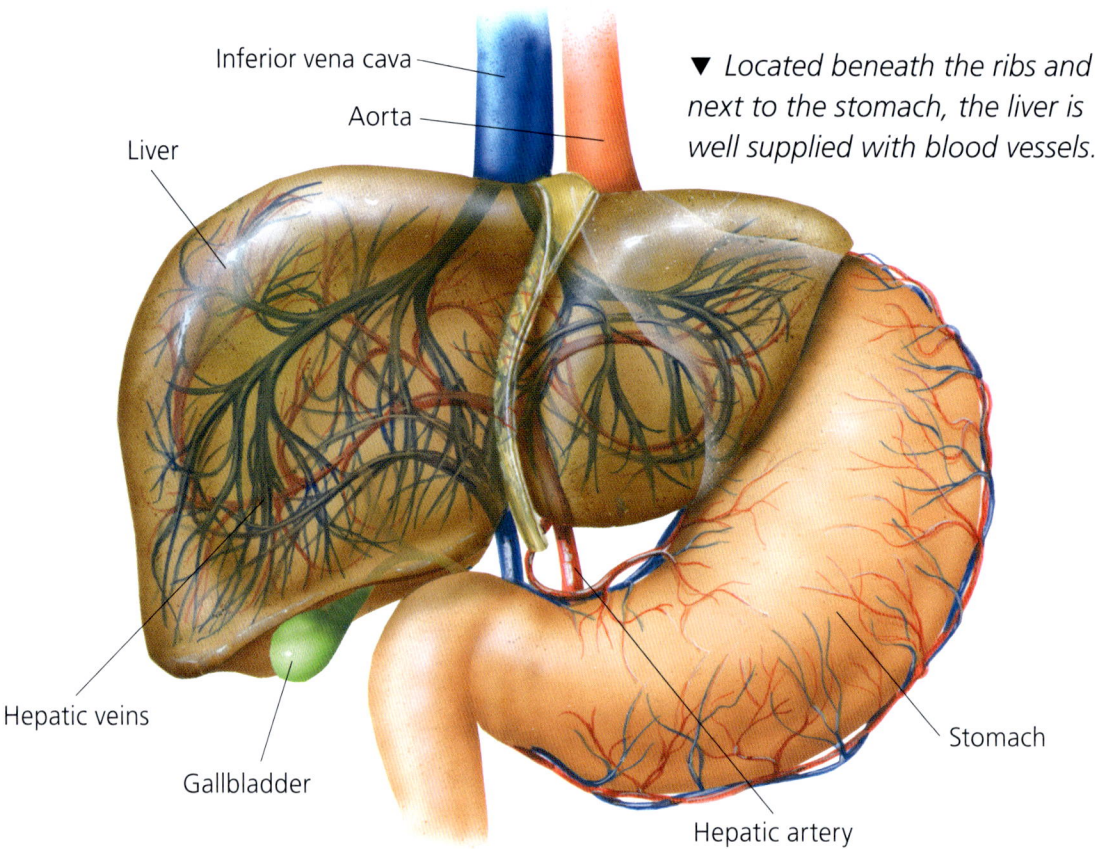

Inferior vena cava

Aorta

Liver

▼ *Located beneath the ribs and next to the stomach, the liver is well supplied with blood vessels.*

Hepatic veins

Gallbladder

Stomach

Hepatic artery

The liver, the largest internal organ, is a chemical processing centre.

The prime task of the liver is to process nutrients and substances digested from food and send them out to body cells, as needed.

The liver turns carbohydrates into glucose, the main energy-giving chemical for the body's cells.

Levels of glucose in the blood are kept steady by the liver. It releases more when levels drop, and stores it as glycogen when levels rise.

Bile is a yellowish or greenish bitter liquid produced by the liver and stored in the gallbladder. It helps to dissolve fat as food is digested.

The liver clears the blood of old red cells and toxic substances, such as alcohol, converting them into less harmful forms.

The pancreas

- The pancreas is a large, carrot-shaped gland that lies just below your stomach.

- Two main types of tissue are contained within the pancreas – one that releases hormones and one that releases pancreatic enzymes.

- The main type of tissue consists of thousands of nests of hormone glands known as the islets of Langerhans.

- The islets of Langerhans release two important hormones: insulin and glucagon.

- The second type of tissue is called exocrine tissue. It secretes (releases) pancreatic enzymes, such as amylase and lipase, into the small intestine to help digest food.

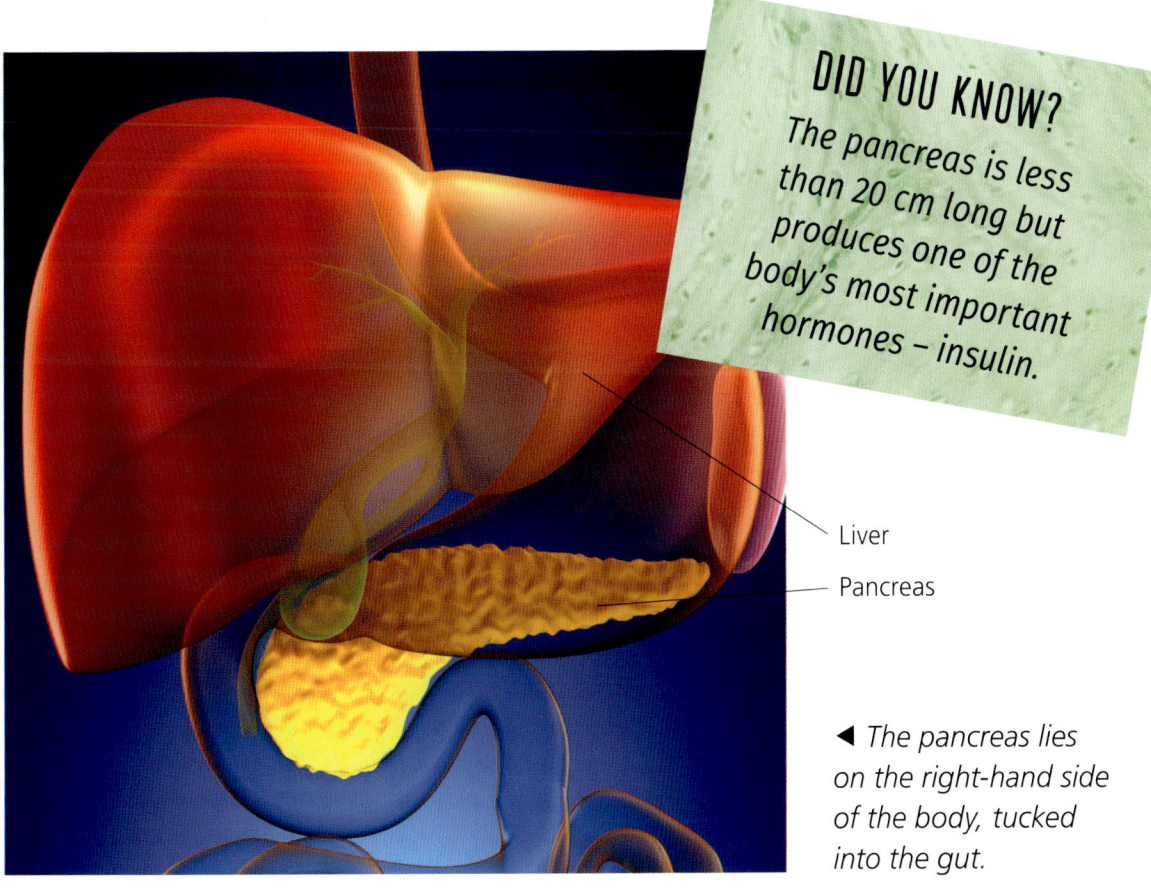

DID YOU KNOW?
The pancreas is less than 20 cm long but produces one of the body's most important hormones – insulin.

Liver

Pancreas

◀ *The pancreas lies on the right-hand side of the body, tucked into the gut.*

103

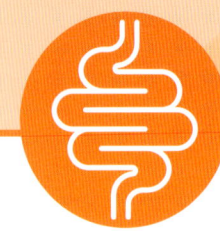

Small intestine

- Once food has been broken down into semi-liquid chyme, by the stomach, it enters the small intestine.

- Your small intestine is a 6-m-long tube that is about 2.5 cm wide.

- The small intestine's lining consists of thousands of folds and tiny projections called villi.

- The first part of the small intestine, the duodenum, mixes the chyme with enzymes and bile to break it down into tiny molecules.

- The middle part of the small intestine, the jejunum, is where food nutrients are absorbed.

- The final part of the small intestine, the ileum, absorbs vitamin B12.

- Once all the useful molecules have been absorbed, the remaining material passes into the large intestine.

Liver

Stomach

Large intestine

Small intestine

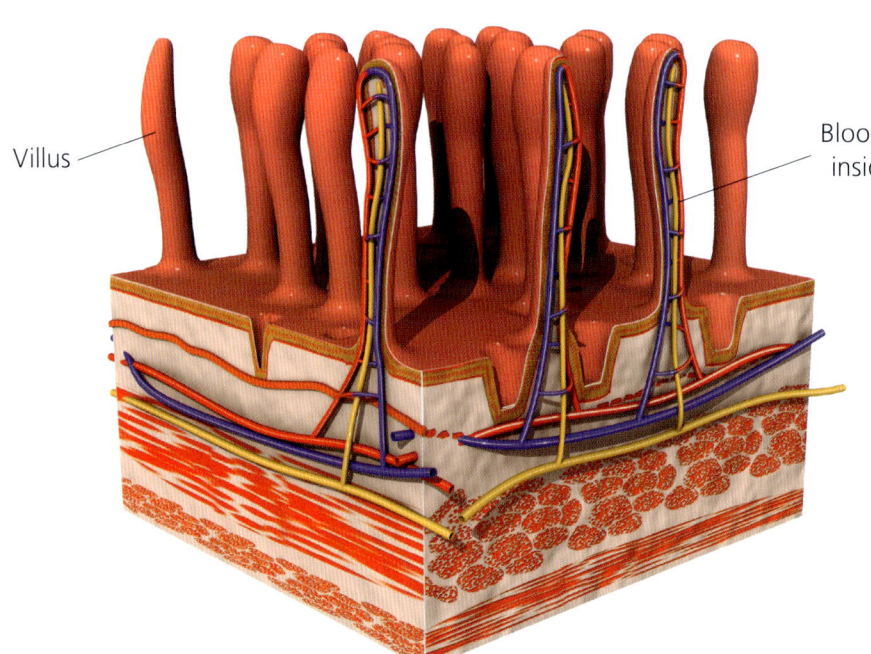

Villus

Blood vessels inside villus

◄ *Each villus has tiny blood vessels that pick up nutrients and carry them away into the bloodstream.*

Large intestine

- The main part of the large intestine is the colon, which is almost as long as you are tall.

- Although it is much wider than the small intestine, the large intestine has a smaller surface area.

- Undigested food in the form of semi-liquid chyme is converted into solid waste by the colon, as it absorbs any excess water.

- The colon soaks up approximately 1.5 litres of water every day.

- Sodium and chlorine are also absorbed by the walls of the colon.

- Billions of bacteria live inside the colon and assist in turning the chyme into your faeces (poo). These bacteria are harmless as long as they do not spread to the rest of the body.

- Bacteria in the colon make the vitamins K and B – as well as smelly gases such as methane and hydrogen sulphide.

- The muscles of the colon break the waste food down into segments, ready for excretion (removal from the body as faeces).

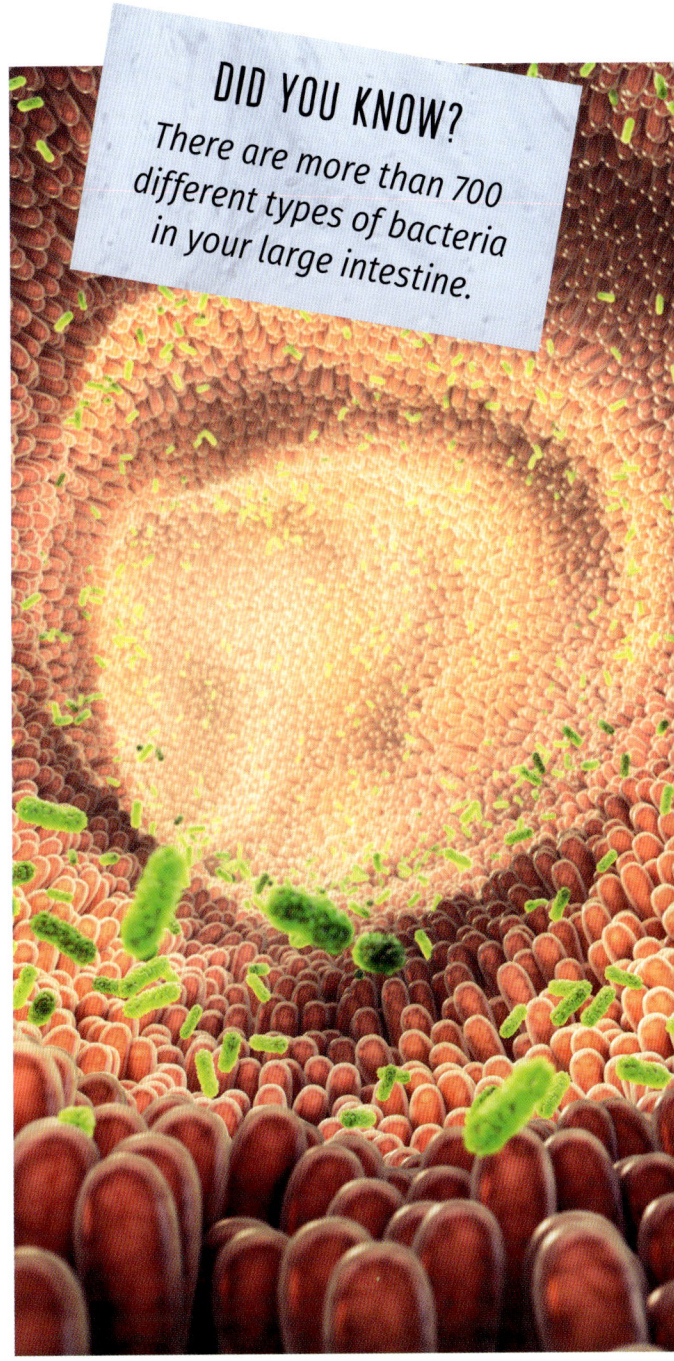

DID YOU KNOW?
There are more than 700 different types of bacteria in your large intestine.

▲ *This computer-generated 3D artwork shows the lumpy lining of the large intestine. The small, green, worm-like objects are 'friendly' bacteria.*

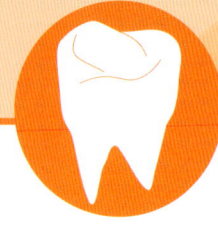

Excretion

- Excretion is the process by which your body gets rid of material (from your food) that it cannot digest.

- Undigested food is prepared for excretion in your large intestine, or bowel.

- Once all the useful molecules and water have been absorbed, the leftover waste leaves the large intestine and collects in your rectum.

- The collection of waste triggers nerve endings in the rectum that make you want to go to the toilet, or defecate.

- The anus is a ring of muscle that relaxes to let out the waste.

- Fibre is essential to keep your gut working properly. Fibre is not absorbed, so it bulks out the waste matter.

- About two-thirds of the waste we produce is water.

- Up to half of the waste material is composed of friendly bacteria that are found in the gut.

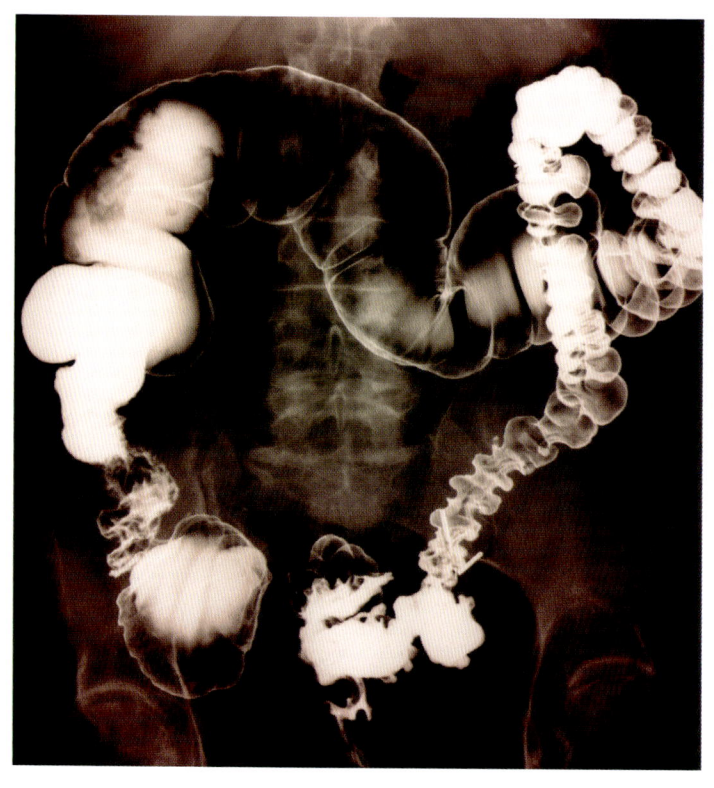

▶ This is an X-ray of the colon. The patient drinks a liquid called barium, which makes the lower intestine show up more clearly in the image, so that doctors can check on its health.

Urinary system

The job of the urinary system is to remove waste products from the blood and from the body.

The kidneys filter the blood to produce urine. This runs down the ureters to collect in the bladder. Urine leaves the body through the urethra.

The urinary system produces about 0.5 to 2 litres of urine every day.

Humans can survive with only one kidney.

▶ *The urinary system consists of a pair of kidneys connected to the bladder and the urethra, a tube that leads to the outside of the body.*

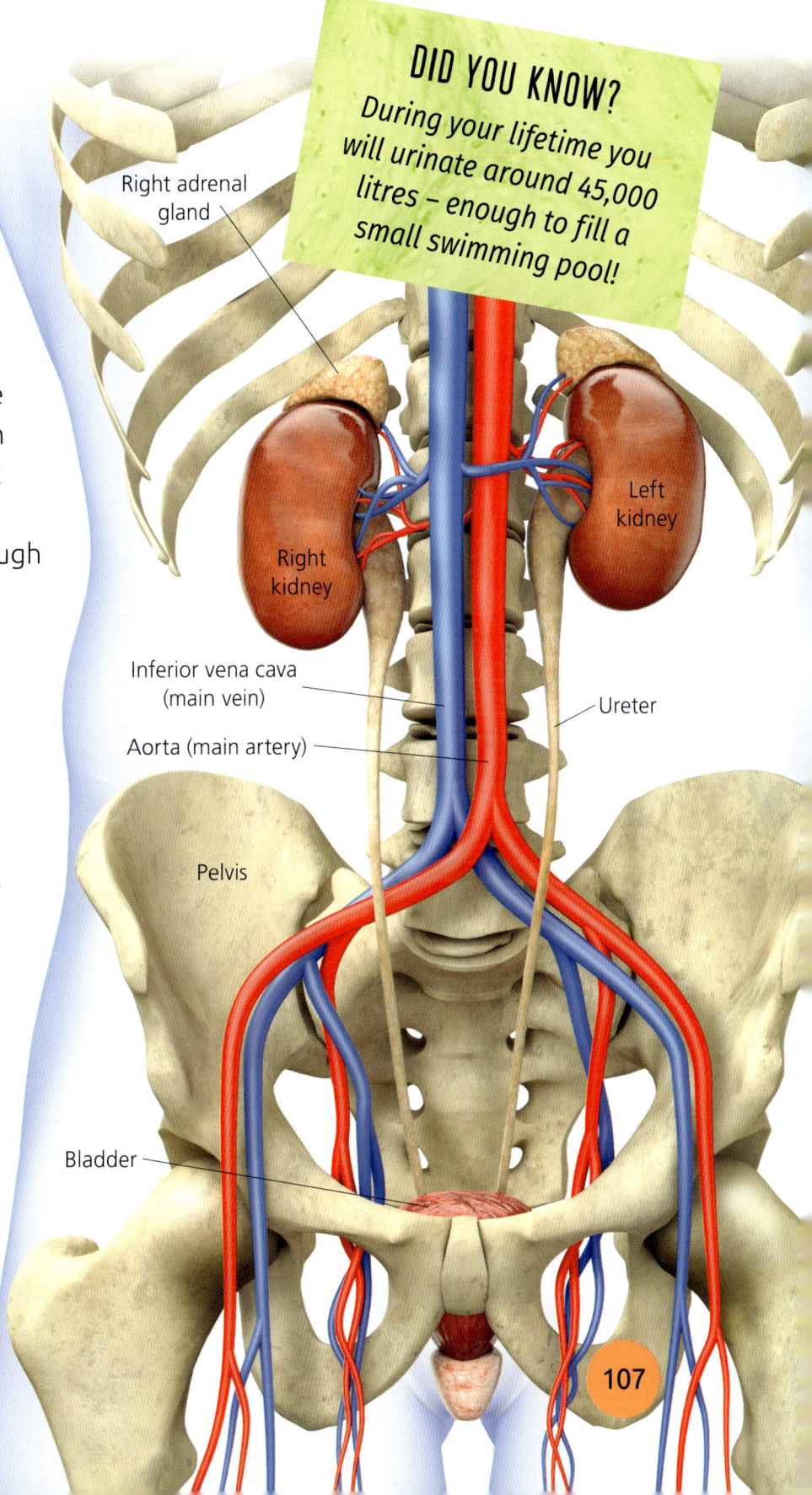

DID YOU KNOW?
During your lifetime you will urinate around 45,000 litres – enough to fill a small swimming pool!

Right adrenal gland

Left kidney

Right kidney

Inferior vena cava (main vein)

Aorta (main artery)

Ureter

Pelvis

Bladder

107

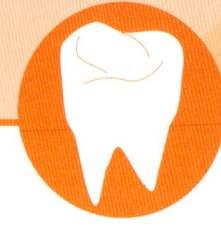

The kidneys

- The kidneys are the body's water control and blood-cleaning plants. They draw off water and important substances from the blood. They then release any unwanted water and waste substances.

- About 1.3 litres of blood are filtered by the kidneys every minute.

- All of the body's blood flows through the kidneys every ten minutes, which means your blood is filtered about 150 times a day.

- The kidneys manage to recycle or save many reusable substances from the blood.

- The kidneys save nearly all of the amino acids and glucose from the blood, as well as 70 per cent of the salt.

- Blood entering each kidney is filtered through a million or more filtration units called nephrons.

- Each nephron is an incredibly intricate network of little pipes called convoluted tubules, wrapped around countless tiny capillaries. Useful blood substances are filtered into the tubules, then reabsorbed back into the blood in the capillaries.

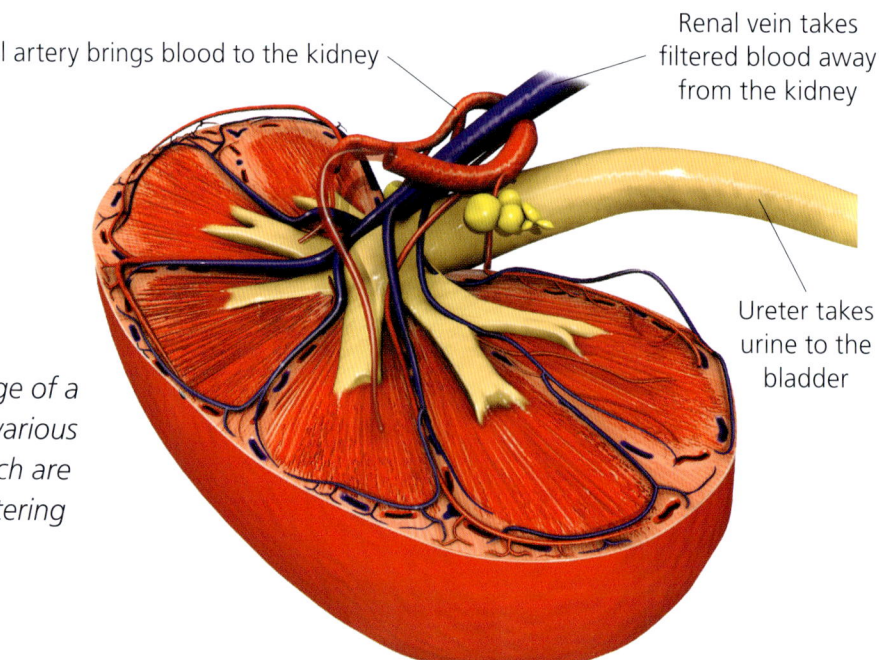

Renal artery brings blood to the kidney

Renal vein takes filtered blood away from the kidney

Ureter takes urine to the bladder

▶ *This close-up cross-section image of a kidney shows its various components, which are responsible for filtering blood and urine.*

The bladder

- The bladder is a hollow, muscular organ that sits deep within the pelvis.

- It acts as a collection bag for the urine produced by the kidneys.

- Urine flows down the two ureters and into the bladder.

- The wall of the bladder is made of smooth muscle and has a highly 'folded' structure.

- As the bladder fills with urine, the folds gradually smooth out so that the bladder can stretch and enlarge its capacity.

- The bladder normally holds up to about 600 ml of urine, but can stretch to hold up to twice this amount if necessary.

- As the bladder stretches, it sends nerve signals to the spinal cord and the brain. These signals tell you that you need to empty your bladder, or urinate.

- We start to feel we need to urinate when the bladder is around a quarter full.

- If we decide to urinate, we relax the muscles at the base of the bladder and within the urethra, so that urine passes out through the urethra.

- At birth, urination is automatic when the bladder is full. As we grow older, we learn to voluntarily control the sphincter muscles around the urethra.

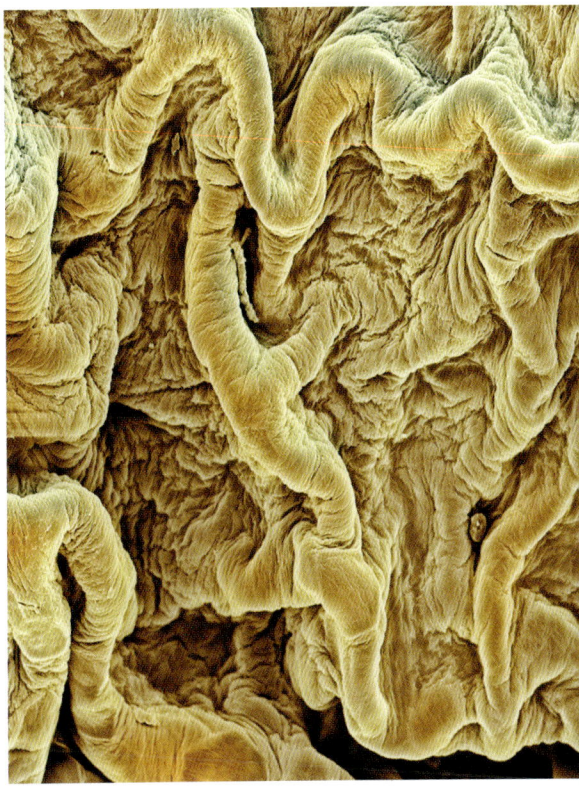

▲ *This highly magnified photograph shows the folded lining of the bladder, which stretches and flattens out as the bladder fills with urine.*

DID YOU KNOW?
Animal bladders have been used to make balls and even musical instruments.

Water

- Water makes up more than 60 per cent of your body.

- You can survive for weeks without food, but no more than a few days without water.

- You gain water by drinking, eating, and as a by-product of cell activity.

- You lose water by sweating, breathing, and in your urine and faeces.

- The average person takes in 2.5 litres of water a day – 1.4 litres in drink and 0.8 litres in food. Body cells provide the remaining 0.3 litres.

- The average person loses 1.5 litres of water every day in urine, 0.5 litres in sweat, 0.3 litres as vapour in exhaled breath, and 0.2 litres in faeces.

- The water balance in the body is controlled mainly by the kidneys and adrenal glands, which sit on top of each kidney.

- The amount of water that the kidneys release in your urine depends on the amount of salt there is in the blood.

- If you drink little or sweat a lot, the blood becomes more salty. The kidneys restore the balance in the blood by holding on to more water.

▶ If you drink a lot, the saltiness of the blood is diluted (watered down). To rebalance it, the kidneys let out a lot of water as urine.

◀ It is important to replace fluid as it is lost, especially if you have been exercising and sweating.

Body salts

▶ *If salty seawater evaporates, salt crystals may appear and accumulate (build up) in shallow pools and on rocks.*

DID YOU KNOW?
The kidneys control the amount of salts and water you have inside your body.

Body salts play an important role in maintaining the balance of water in the body, and on the inside and outside of body cells.

Important minerals and elements in body salts include potassium, sodium, manganese, chloride, carbonate and phosphate.

The hypothalamus (see page 72) monitors salt levels in the blood and sends signals telling the kidneys to either hold on to water or let it go.

You gain salt from the food you eat. Too much salt in food may result in high blood pressure in certain people.

Your body can lose salt if you sweat heavily. This can cause painful muscle 'cramps', which is why people in hot, dry environments – such as deserts – actively replenish (top up) their salt levels.

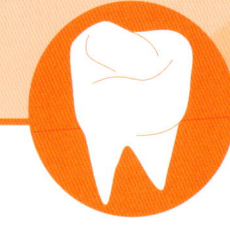

Diet

- Your diet is what you regularly eat. A good diet includes adequate portions of proteins, carbohydrates, fats, vitamins, minerals, fibre and water.

- Most of the food you eat is fuel for the body, provided mostly by carbohydrates and fats.

- Carbohydrates are foods made from types of sugar, as well as complex starches and fibre. Bread, rice, pasta and potatoes are carbohydrates.

- Fats are not usually burned up straightaway, but are stored around your body until they are needed.

- Proteins are needed for building and repairing cells. They are made from special chemicals called amino acids.

- Fibre, or roughage, is supplied by cellulose from the walls of plant cells. Your body cannot digest fibre, but needs it for 'bulk' to keep the bowel muscles well exercised.

Bread, other cereals and potatoes

Fruits and vegetables

Meat, fish and their alternatives

Foods that contain fat or sugar

Milk and dairy foods

▲ *This diagram shows the types and proportions of different foods that make up a healthy diet.*

Fats

- Fats are an important source of energy.

- While carbohydrates are generally used for 'immediate' energy, your body often stores fat to use for energy in times of shortage.

- Weight for weight, fats contain twice as much energy as carbohydrates.

- Fats are important organic (life) substances, found in almost every living thing. They are composed of substances called fatty acids and glycerol.

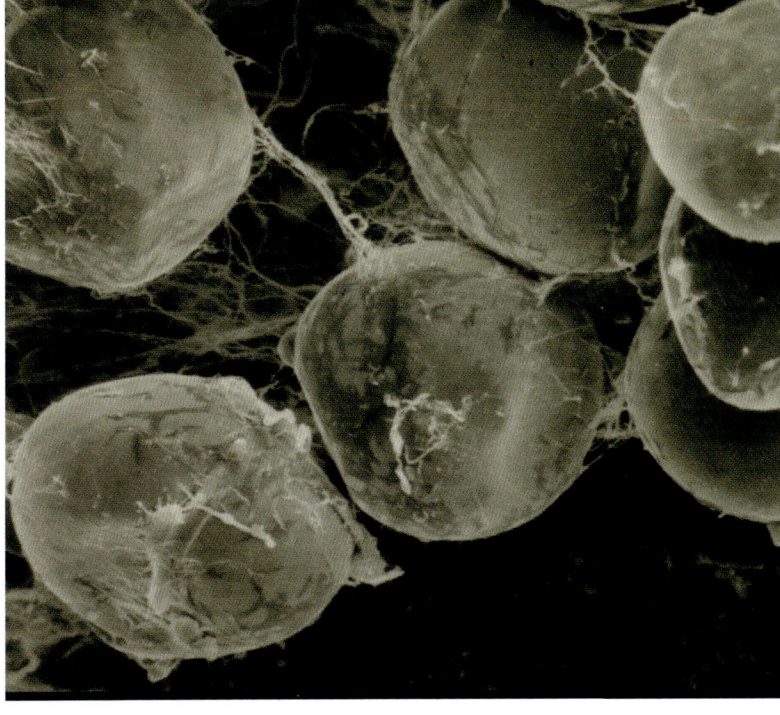

▲ *Fat cells are numerous under the skin, providing your body with a store of energy and a layer of insulation to keep in warmth.*

- Food fats are greasy vegetable or animal fats that will not dissolve in water. Some, such as the fats in meat and cheese, are solid. Some, such as cooking oils, are liquid.

▶ *Cheese contains saturated fat, which is linked to high levels of the substance cholesterol in the blood – and may increase the risk of a heart attack.*

DID YOU KNOW?
There are two main types of fat – saturated and unsaturated.

113

Carbohydrates

Carbohydrates in food represent the body's main source of energy. They are plentiful in sweet things and in starchy foods such as bread, cakes and potatoes.

DID YOU KNOW?
Carbohydrates should make up about half of your diet.

Carbohydrates are burned by the body in order to keep it warm and to provide energy for growth and muscle movement, as well as to maintain basic body processes.

Carbohydrates are among the most common of organic (life) substances. Plants use the energy in sunlight to make their chemical energy, which is stored as carbohydrates.

Chemical substances called sugars are also carbohydrates. Sucrose (found in sugar lumps and caster sugar) is just one of these sugars.

Simple carbohydrates such as glucose, fructose (the sweetness in fruit) and sucrose are sweet and dissolve in water.

Carbohydrates are turned into glucose for your body to use straightaway, or stored in the liver as the complex sugar glycogen (body starch).

◄ *Rice, potatoes, bread and other wheat products are all full of starch, a complex carbohydrate that gives us a steady supply of energy.*

Glucose

- After a meal, glucose travels in the blood from the small intestine to the liver, where excess is stored in the form of starchy glycogen.

- For your body to work effectively, levels of glucose in the blood (known as your blood sugar) must always be correct.

- Glucose is the body's energy chemical, used as fuel in all cell activity.

- Glucose is a type of sugar made by plants as they take energy from sunlight. It is commonly found in many fruits, along with fructose.

- The body gets its glucose from carbohydrates in food, broken down in stages in the small intestine.

- Blood sugar levels are controlled by two hormones, glucagon and insulin, which are sent out by the pancreas.

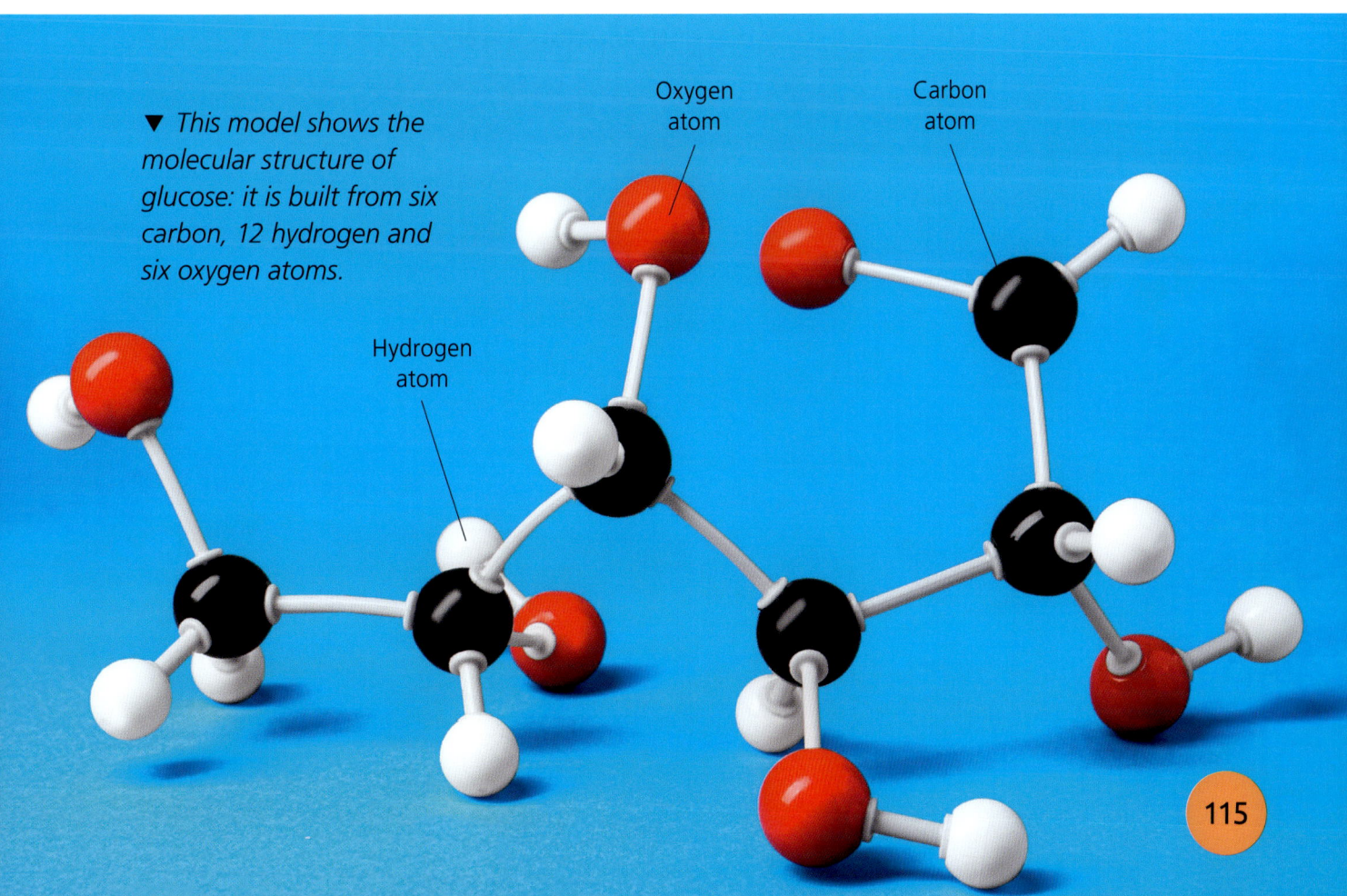

▼ *This model shows the molecular structure of glucose: it is built from six carbon, 12 hydrogen and six oxygen atoms.*

Oxygen atom

Carbon atom

Hydrogen atom

Proteins

For its growth and repair, the body needs proteins.

Proteins from food are broken down in the body into amino acids. These are then used to make new, different proteins within the body.

There are 20 different amino acids. Your body can make 11 of them. The other nine are called essential acids and they come from food.

Foods that are high in protein include meat, fish, eggs, milk, cheese, nuts, lentils and beans.

About one-sixth of a healthy diet should consist of protein.

▲ Vegetarians do not eat meat or fish, so they need to consume enough alternative sources of protein, such as chickpeas.

▼ Nuts, such as these almonds, are good sources of protein. They also contain vitamins and minerals.

▲ Meat, fish, eggs and dairy products, such as milk and cheese, are our most common sources of protein.

Fibre

- Fibre is material in food that the body cannot break down.

- Partly digested food in the gut is given bulk by fibre, making it easier for the food to move along it.

- Fibre also softens partly digested food, making it easier to excrete.

- Fibre generally passes out of the body undigested.

- There are two types of fibre – soluble fibre (dissolves in water) and insoluble fibre (does not dissolve in water).

- Soluble fibre is found in oats, some fruits and vegetables, and in various beans and pulses.

- Insoluble fibre is found in whole grains, wheat, nuts, seeds and some vegetables.

▼ *Beans, bananas, seeds and nuts are all good sources of fibre.*

DID YOU KNOW?
Most of us eat far less fibre than we should – adults need about 18 g per day.

▲ *Peanuts contain a surprising amount of fibre, as well as healthy fats and protein.*

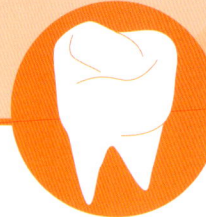

Vitamins

- Vitamins are special substances the body needs to help maintain chemical processes inside cells.

- There are 13 'essential' vitamins. A lack of any vitamin in the diet can cause certain illnesses.

- Some vitamins – such as A, D, E and K – dissolve in fat and are found in animal fats and vegetable oils. They may be stored in the body for months.

- Vitamin C is found in fruits such as oranges and tomatoes, and in fresh green vegetables.

- There are several B vitamins. These dissolve in water and are found in green leaves, fruits and cereal grains. Many are also present in meat and fish. They are used daily by the body.

- Vitamin D and some forms of vitamin K are made inside the body. K is made by bacteria in the gut.

- Vitamin D is made in the skin when we are out in the sun; it is essential for bone growth in children.

▼ *Citrus fruits – such as oranges, lemons and limes – and green vegetables are full of vitamins, which is why they are so important in our diet.*

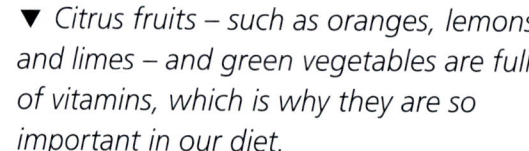

Minerals

- Minerals are substances that are needed to keep the body functioning healthily.

- You require at least 15 'essential' minerals. Most minerals are simple chemical elements, such as calcium and potassium.

- Day to day, you only need to consume tiny amounts of each mineral, but without them you are likely to become ill.

- Your body can store some minerals, such as calcium, but needs a regular supply of others from your food.

- A healthy, balanced diet – including plenty of fruit and vegetables – should supply all the minerals that your body needs.

- Iron can be found in meat, eggs and leafy green vegetables. You need iron to help the body create red blood cells.

- Calcium helps to build strong bones and teeth. It is found in dairy products such as milk and cheese – and in fish with bones, such as sardines.

- Healthy bones also require magnesium, which is found in nuts, seafood and cocoa.

▲ *Spinach is a good source of iron.*

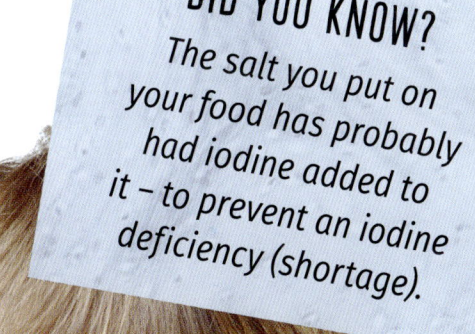

DID YOU KNOW?
The salt you put on your food has probably had iodine added to it – to prevent an iodine deficiency (shortage).

▶ *Many toothpastes contain the mineral fluoride, which helps to strengthen your teeth and prevent tooth decay.*

The endocrine system

- Many bodily functions are controlled by dedicated chemicals called hormones.

- Hormones are produced by a number of specialized glands called endocrine glands.

- Endocrine glands are also known as ductless glands because they release their secretions directly into the blood and not into a duct (tube) like other types of glands do (the salivary glands, for example).

- These glands include the thyroid gland, the pancreas, the pituitary gland, the adrenal glands, the testes, the ovaries and the parathyroid glands.

- Most hormones are proteins, but some are classed as steroids.

▶ *Endocrine glands are situated all over the body. Each hormone affects only certain body parts, known as target organs.*

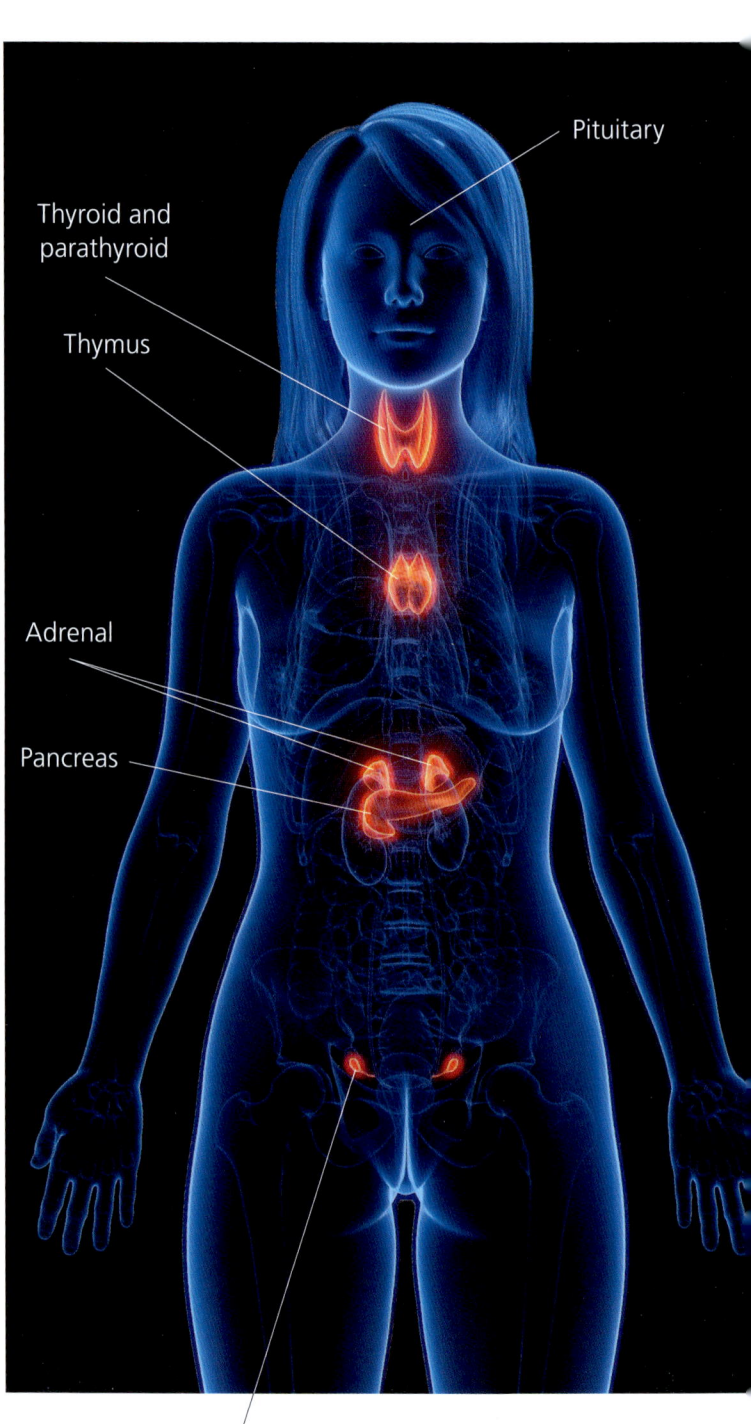

Thyroid and parathyroid

Thymus

Adrenal

Pancreas

Pituitary

Sex hormones – ovaries in females (shown here), testes in males

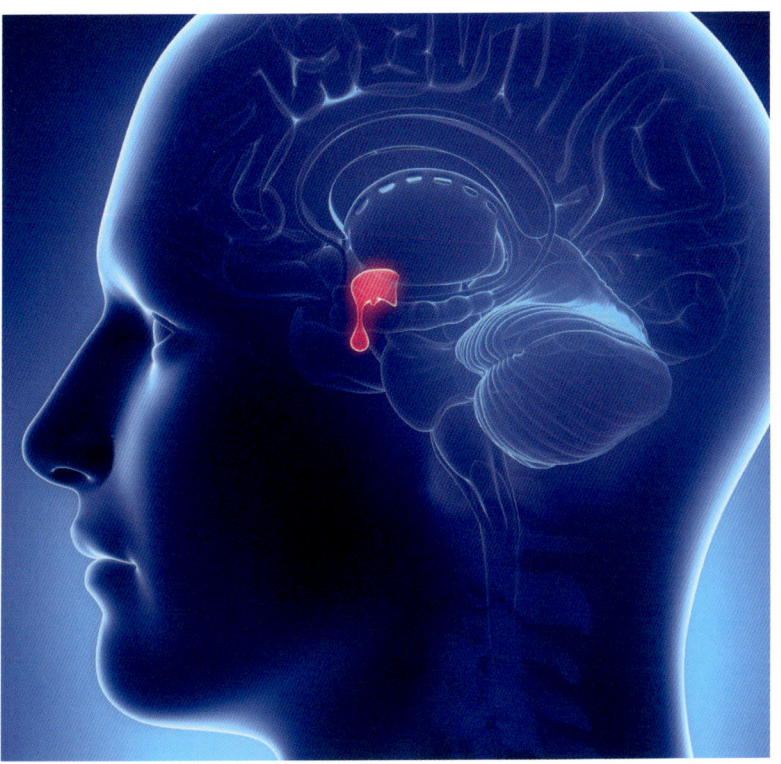

◄ *The pituitary gland (highlighted in pink) releases eight different hormones. They control major developments in the body such as growth and reproduction.*

The effect of the hormones produced by the endocrine system is usually quite far away from the site of release.

The pituitary gland is located at the base of the brain, sitting in a cup-shaped depression in the skull called the sella turcica.

The pituitary and hypothalamus work together – and they produce the largest number of different hormones.

The parathyroid glands are embedded in the back of the thyroid gland, in the neck, which is itself an endocrine gland.

The pancreas is unusual as it is both an endocrine (hormone-producing) gland and an exocrine gland, manufacturing chemicals that it secretes into a duct.

The thymus gland is active only in childhood. It helps the immune (infection-fighting) system to develop.

DID YOU KNOW?
The pineal gland sets your body's clock by releasing melatonin, a hormone that makes you feel drowsy.

Hormones

🖐 Hormones are the body's chemical messengers, released from glands at specific times to trigger reactions in different parts of the body.

🖐 Most hormones are endocrine hormones that are spread around the body by your bloodstream.

🖐 Hormones are controlled by feedback systems. This means they are only released when their 'store' gets the right trigger – which may be a chemical in the blood or another hormone.

🖐 Major hormone sources include the pituitary gland, the thyroid gland, the adrenal glands, the pancreas, a woman's ovaries and a man's testes.

🖐 Some hormones only work on certain cells in the body. Others work throughout the body.

🖐 Endorphins and enkephalins block or relieve pain.

🖐 Oestrogen and progesterone are female sex hormones that control a woman's monthly egg-releasing cycle.

🖐 Testosterone is a male sex hormone that controls the workings of a man's sex organs.

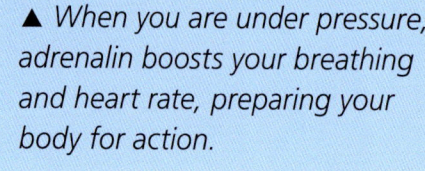

▲ *When you are under pressure, adrenalin boosts your breathing and heart rate, preparing your body for action.*

DID YOU KNOW?
As you get older, the levels of hormones in your body change.

Puberty

- Puberty is the stage in life when children mature 'sexually'. The age of puberty varies, but on average it begins between 11 and 13 years.

- There are three main types of sex hormones: androgens, oestrogens and progesterones.

- Androgens are male hormones such as testosterone.

- Oestrogen is the female hormone made mainly in the ovaries. It causes sexual organs to develop and controls the menstrual cycle.

- Progesterone is the female hormone that prepares the uterus (womb) for pregnancy (growing a baby) every month.

- Primary sexual characteristics are the internal organs that indicate whether someone is male or female – the ovaries and uterus in a girl, and the testes and prostate gland in a boy.

- Secondary sexual characteristics are external differences that develop during puberty to indicate whether someone is male or female. A girl's breasts develop; hair grows under her arms and around her genitals. Hair grows on a boy's face, under his arms and around his genitals.

Gland produces sebum   Sebum   Pore becomes blocked   Spot forms

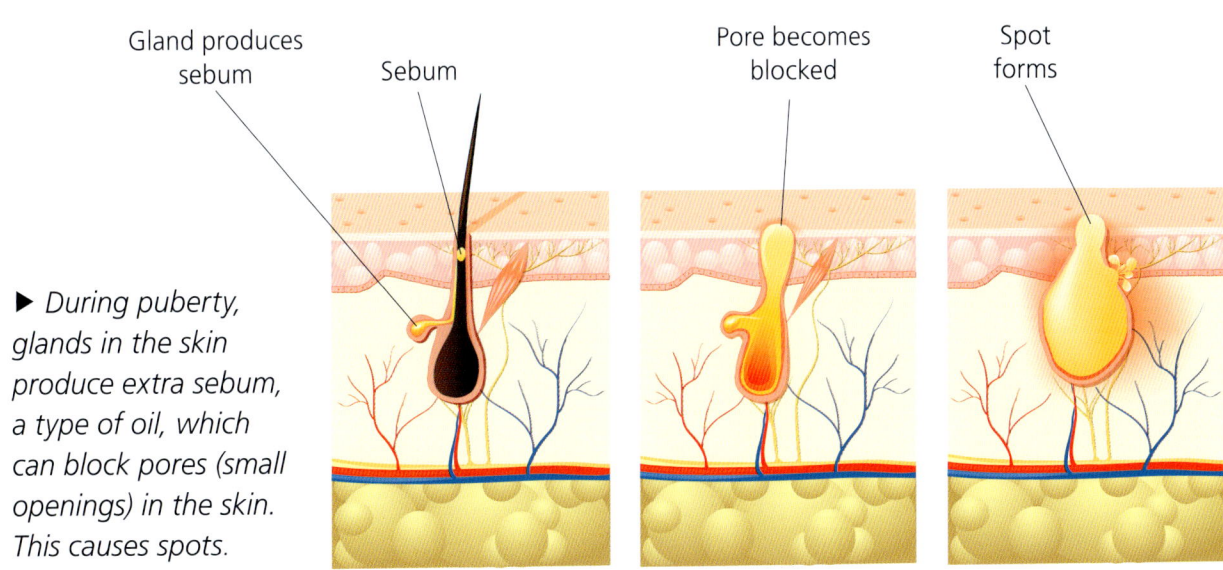

▶ *During puberty, glands in the skin produce extra sebum, a type of oil, which can block pores (small openings) in the skin. This causes spots.*

123

The reproductive systems

- The female reproductive system consists of the uterus (womb) fallopian tubes, ovaries, cervix and vagina.

- A woman's reproductive system is where her body stores and releases the egg cells that create a new human life with a male sperm cell.

- Eggs are gradually released from the ovaries until menopause, which usually occurs when a woman is between 45 and 55 years of age.

- The female reproductive system also produces sex hormones needed for the menstrual cycle – and for a girl to develop at puberty.

- The male reproductive system consists of the penis, scrotum and the two testes (singular: testis).

- A male reproductive system is where the body creates the sperm cells that combine with a female egg cell to create a new human life.

- Sperm cells look like microscopically tiny tadpoles. They are created in the testes, which are inside the scrotum.

- Sperm leave the testes via the epididymis – a thin, coiled tube that is about 6 m long.

- The male reproductive system also produces sex hormones that are needed for the production of sperm – and for a boy to develop at puberty.

- The male sex hormone testosterone also stimulates bone and muscle growth.

▶ *A mature sperm cell consists of a head (where the genetic information is stored), a midsection and a tadpole-like tail.*

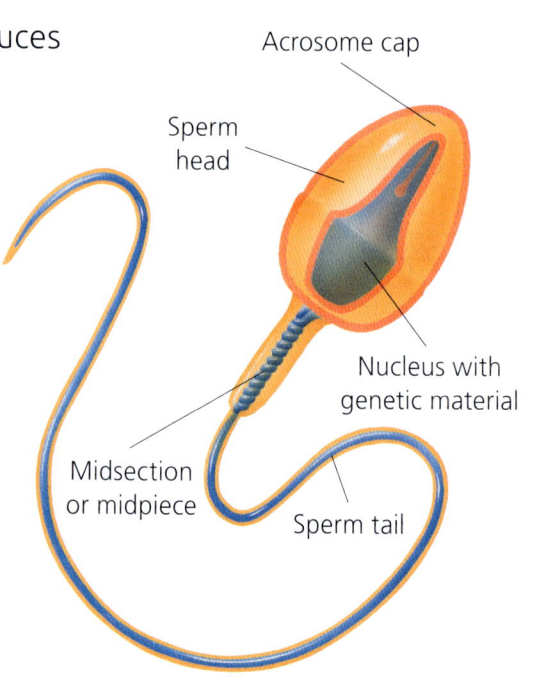

Acrosome cap

Sperm head

Nucleus with genetic material

Midsection or midpiece

Sperm tail

The menstrual cycle

- The menstrual cycle prepares a woman's body for pregnancy.

- Once puberty has begun, it takes place roughly every four weeks and continues until the menopause, when hormone levels suddenly drop.

- Eggs in the ovaries are stored in follicles. A monthly menstrual cycle begins when the follicle-stimulating hormone (FSH) is sent by the pituitary gland in the brain to spur one of the follicles to grow.

- As the follicle grows, it releases the sex hormone oestrogen. Oestrogen makes the lining of the uterus (womb) thicken.

- Halfway through the menstrual cycle, luteinizing hormone (LH) from the pituitary gland makes the follicle rupture, and an egg is released.

- The empty egg follicle starts to produce progesterone, which also thickens the lining of the uterus.

- One egg cell is released each menstrual cycle by one of the two ovaries.

- The egg travels down one of the fallopian tubes to the uterus.

- If the egg is not fertilized, it is shed, along with the womb lining, in a flow of blood and tissue from the vagina. This shedding is known as a menstrual period.

▶ *This illustration shows a magnified view of an ovum (egg cell) leaving the ovary and travelling down the fallopian tube.*

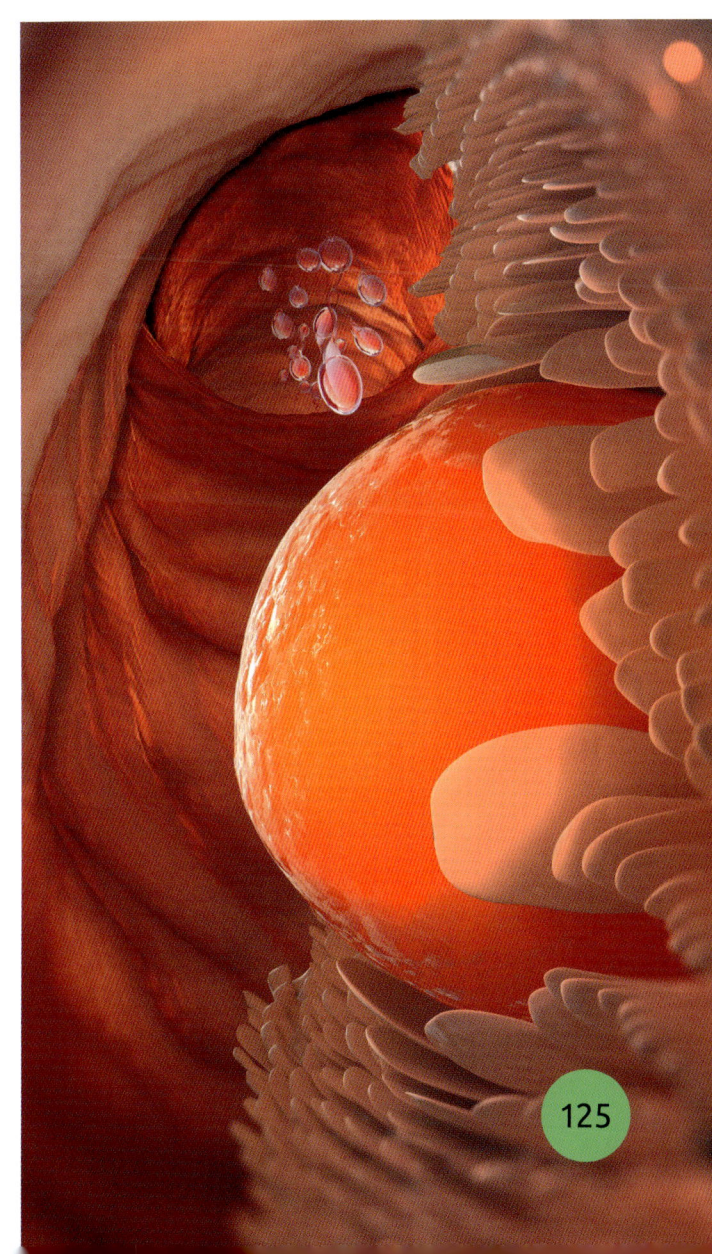

125

Reproduction

- Reproduction occurs when a developed egg meets a sperm cell during sexual intercourse.

- If a man and woman have sexual intercourse, the penis is stimulated. Sperm are driven into a tube called the vas deferens and mix with a liquid called seminal fluid to make semen.

- Semen shoots through the urethra (the tube inside the penis through which males urinate) and is ejaculated into the female's vagina.

- The sperm from the man's penis may swim up the woman's vagina, enter her womb and fertilize the egg in the fallopian tube.

- Although millions of sperm cells are usually released, only one is needed to fertilize the egg.

- If the egg is fertilized, the womb lining continues to thicken, ready for pregnancy, instead of being shed during a menstrual period.

- The fertilized egg implants itself into the thick lining of the womb and carries on developing. It is now an embryo – a very tiny baby.

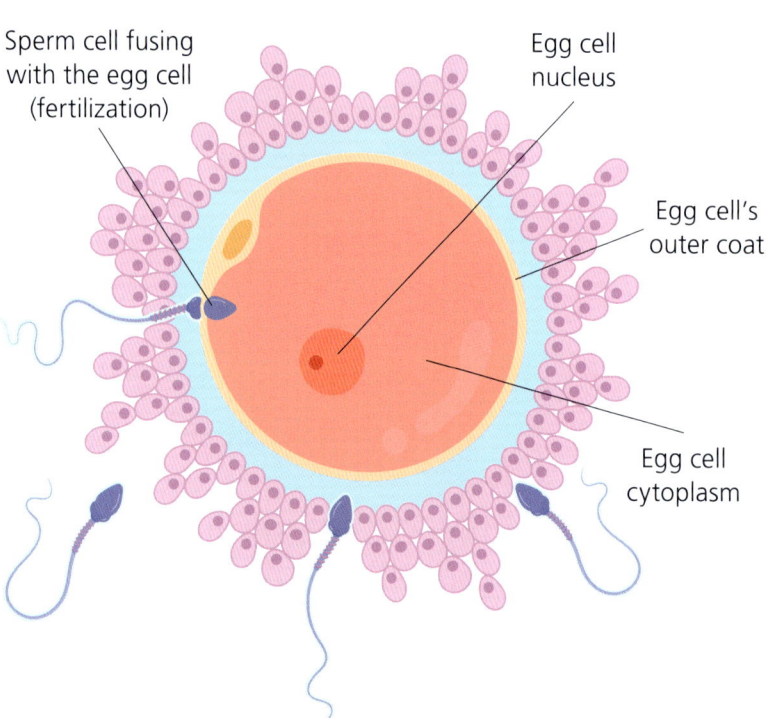

Sperm cell fusing with the egg cell (fertilization)

Egg cell nucleus

Egg cell's outer coat

Egg cell cytoplasm

◄ *Only one single sperm will be successful in penetrating the egg's outer layers, using enzymes, which causes its genetic material to combine with the egg's genetic material. This process forms a single cell called a zygote – the fertilized egg.*

Pregnancy

- Pregnancy begins when a woman's ovum (egg cell) is fertilized by a man's sperm cell.

- When a woman becomes pregnant, her monthly menstrual periods stop. Blood and urine tests can confirm the pregnancy.

- During pregnancy, the fertilized egg cell divides again and again to grow rapidly – first into an embryo (first eight weeks) and then into a foetus (eight weeks until birth).

- Unlike an embryo, a foetus has developed legs and arms, as well as internal organs such as a heart.

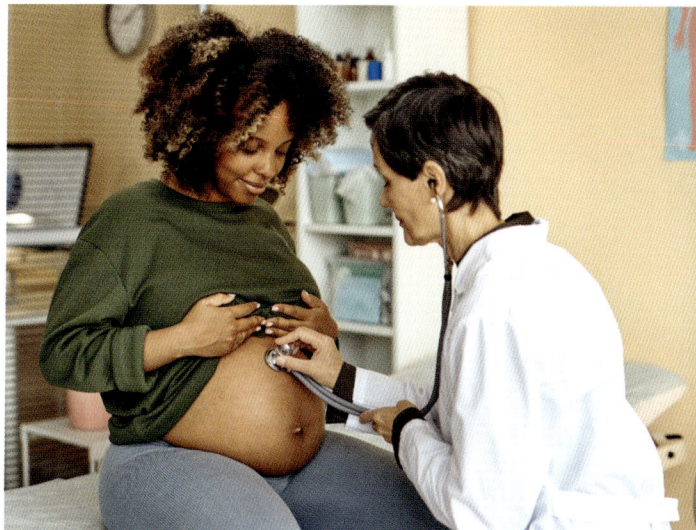

▲ *Pregnant women are advised to have between seven and ten check-ups during this time, to monitor their health and that of their unborn baby.*

- The average pregnancy lasts about 40 weeks, which is divided into three 'trimesters': weeks 1–13, weeks 14–27 and weeks 28–40.

- The foetus lies cushioned in its mother's uterus (womb), inside a bag of fluid called the amniotic sac.

- From around weeks 16–20 of pregnancy, the foetus develops a soft, fine covering of hair called lanugo, normally shed in weeks 32–36.

- The mother's blood passes food and oxygen to the foetus via the placenta, which emerges as the 'afterbirth' when the baby is born.

- The umbilical cord runs between the foetus and the placenta, transporting blood to and from the developing infant.

- During her pregnancy, a woman gains around 30 per cent more blood, and her heart rate increases.

Birth

- A baby is considered 'full-term' in weeks 37 to 42 of a pregnancy.

- A few weeks or days before a baby is born, it usually turns in the uterus (womb) so that its head is pointing downwards, in the pelvis, towards the mother's birth canal (her cervix and vagina).

- Birth begins as the mother goes into labour. This is when the womb muscles begin a rhythm of contracting (tightening) and relaxing in order to push the baby out through the birth canal.

- In the first stage of labour, the womb muscles contract and burst the bag of fluid around the baby. The fluid drains out through the vagina.

- In the second stage of labour, the baby is pushed out through the birth canal, usually head first.

- In the third stage of labour, the placenta – which delivers oxygen and nutrients to the baby from the mother's blood – is shed and comes out through the birth canal as the 'afterbirth'.

- The umbilical cord (connecting the baby to the placenta) is cut after birth – but not always straightaway! Cutting the cord is often delayed, so that the baby can receive blood, iron and vital stem cells from the placenta during its first few minutes of life outside of the womb.

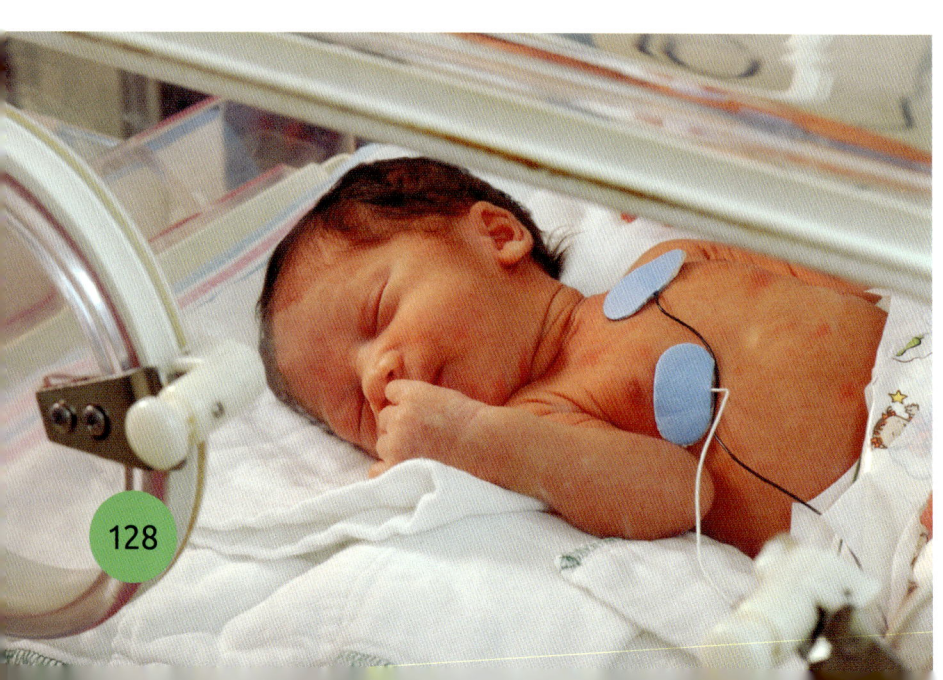

◀ Babies that weigh less than 2.5 kg are considered to have 'low birth weight'. This is often the result of a 'premature' birth (before week 37 of pregnancy). Premature infants are nursed in special care units.

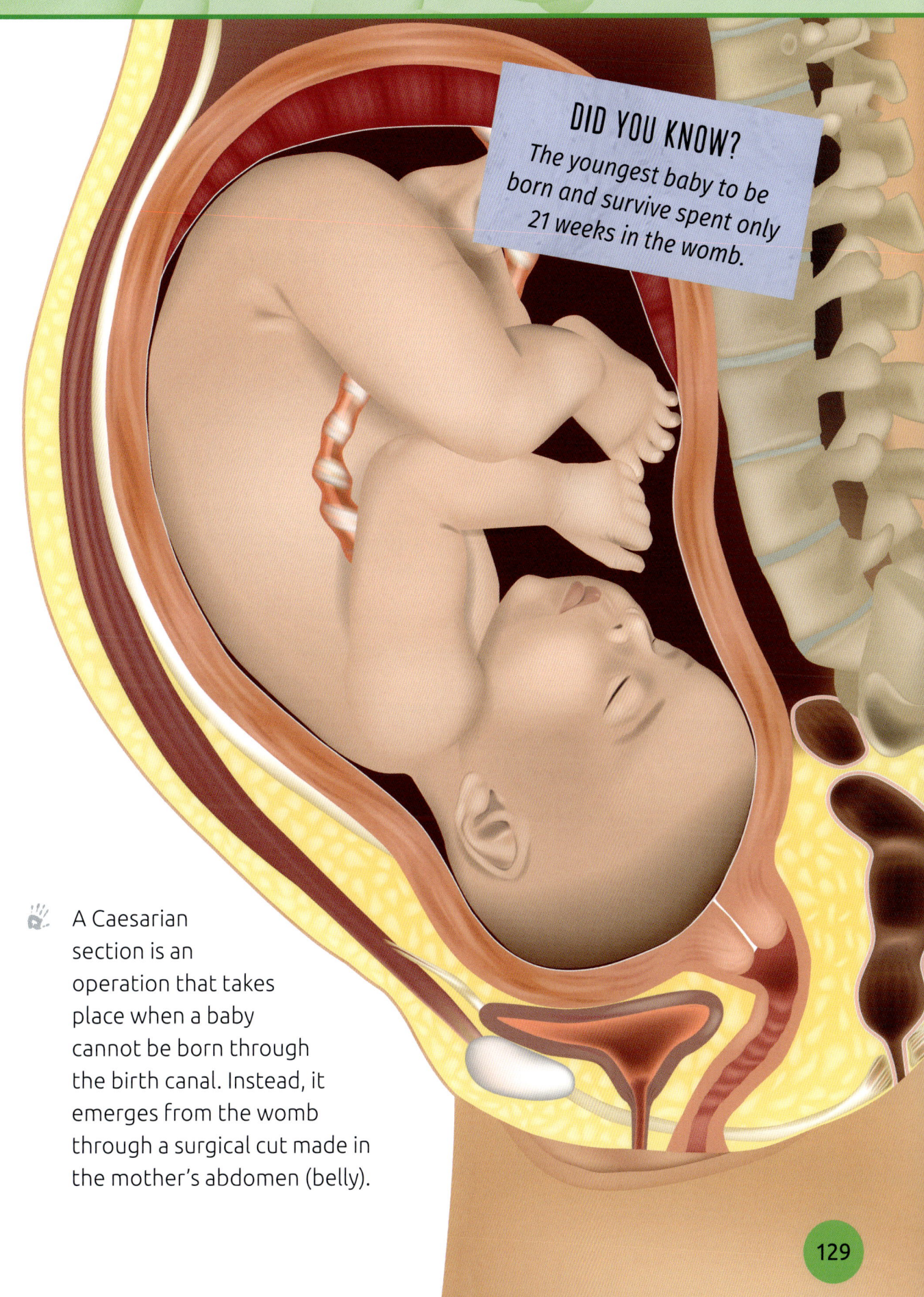

DID YOU KNOW?
The youngest baby to be born and survive spent only 21 weeks in the womb.

A Caesarian section is an operation that takes place when a baby cannot be born through the birth canal. Instead, it emerges from the womb through a surgical cut made in the mother's abdomen (belly).

129

Babies

- Newborn babies usually weigh 3–4 kg and are about 50 cm in length.

- A baby's head is approximately a quarter of its total body length. Its head will be about four times bigger by the time it reaches adulthood.

- A baby's skeleton is fairly soft and flexible, to allow for growth. The cartilage in the skeleton 'ossifies' (hardens into solid bone) over time.

- There are two 'soft spots' – called fontanelles – between the bones of a baby's skull, where there is only membrane (a 'skin' of thin tissue) instead of solid bone. These areas close up and the bones fuse, or join together, by around 18 months of age.

- A baby has a gland called the thymus gland at the centre of its chest, behind the breastbone. This gland provides vital immunity against infection – but gradually shrinks after the child reaches puberty.

- A baby has a very developed sense of taste, with taste buds all over the inside of its mouth.

- Babies have a much stronger sense of smell than adults do – perhaps to help them pick up the familiar scent of their mothers.

▼ *A newborn baby cannot hold up its head, so it must always be supported with care.*

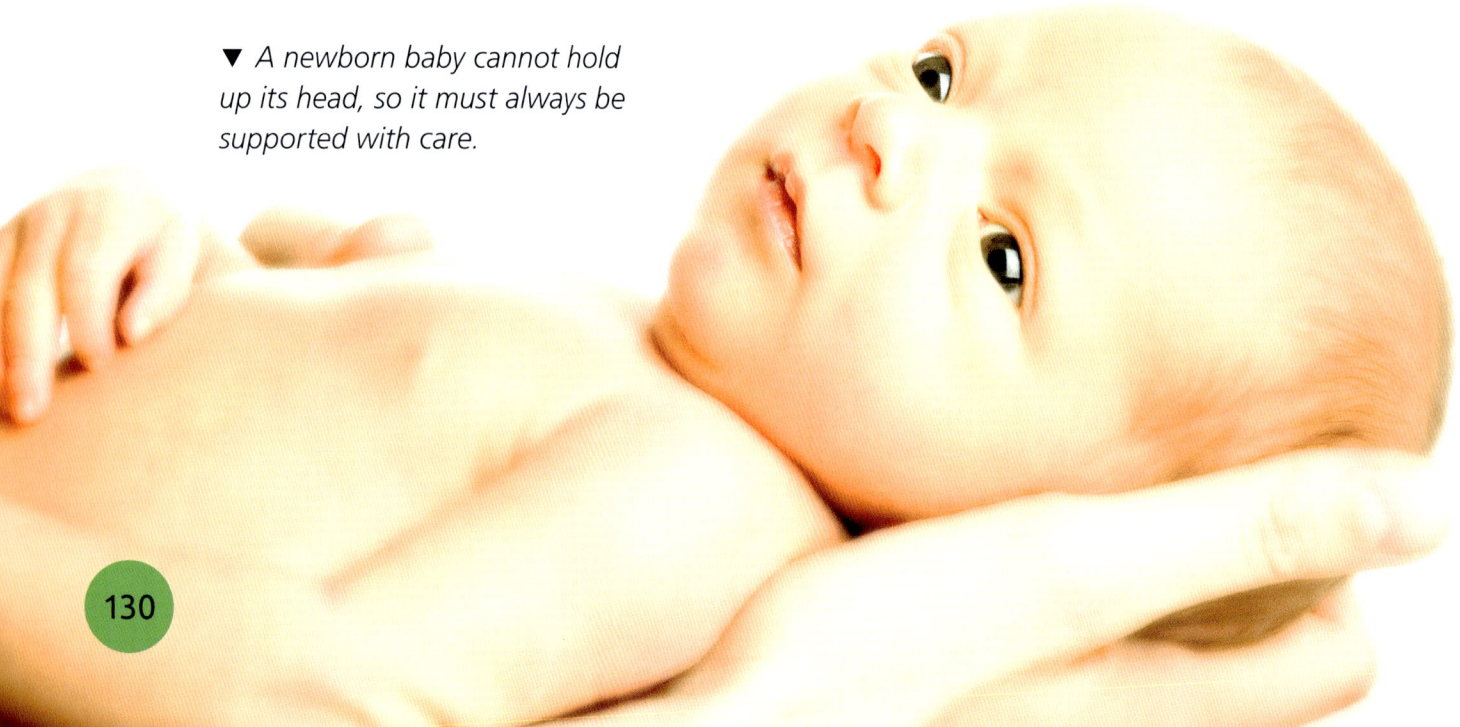

◀ *Babies normally begin to smile between 6 and 12 weeks old.*

DID YOU KNOW?
A baby's body weight usually triples during the first year of its life.

- A baby's eyesight is poor to begin with and its eyelids are usually puffy.

- A baby is born with primitive reflexes (things it does automatically) such as grasping or sucking a person's finger.

- A baby seems to learn to control its body in stages, starting first with its head, then moving on to its arms and legs.

- Body proportions change as we grow. A baby's legs make up only around one-quarter of its length, but by the time we are fully grown our legs make up almost half of our total height.

- Growth is controlled by hormones, especially 'growth hormone', which is produced by the pituitary gland in the brain.

Childhood milestones

- The development of movement and learning is different in all infants, but by six to ten months, many may be crawling and pulling themselves upright.

- Toddlers may start walking at any time from nine to 18 months.

- At 12 months onwards we begin to scribble, and by the age of three many infants can draw a straight line.

- We usually say our first word at around 12 to 14 months old, and start to put words together between 14 months and two years old.

- Many children can talk in sentences by three-and-a-half years old and learn to read between five and six years old.

- Typically, by five years old children can talk, walk, run, play, eat, dress and make friends.

DID YOU KNOW?
You learn faster in the first few years of your life than at any other time.

▶ *Toddlers begin to grasp objects at about eight months old and may be able to build a tower from around 18 months onwards.*

Ageing

- Most people live for between 60 and 100 years, but some do live even longer than this.

- The longest officially confirmed age is that of Jeanne Calment, a French woman who died in 1997, aged 122 years and 164 days.

- In Europe, on average, men reach an age of 79 years, while women live to around 84.

- As adults grow older, their bodies begin to deteriorate (fail). Senses such as hearing, sight and taste weaken.

- Hair goes grey as pigment (colour) cells stop working.

- Muscles weaken as their fibres die.

- Bones become more brittle as they lose calcium. Cartilage shrinks between joints, causing stiffness.

▲ *Improvements in health standards mean that more and more people than ever before are remaining physically fit in their old age.*

DID YOU KNOW?
In the UK, there are more people aged over 60 than there are aged under 16.

- Skin wrinkles as the rubbery elastin and collagen fibres that support it sag. Exposure to sunlight speeds up this process, which is why the face and hands get wrinkles first.

- Circulation and breathing weaken. Blood vessels may become stiff and clogged, forcing the heart to work harder and raising blood pressure.

Types of disease

A disease is something that upsets the normal working of any living thing. It can be acute (sudden, but short-lived), chronic (long-lasting), malignant (spreading) or benign (not spreading).

Some diseases are classified by the body part they affect (such as heart disease) or by the body activity they affect, such as a respiratory (breathing-related) disorder.

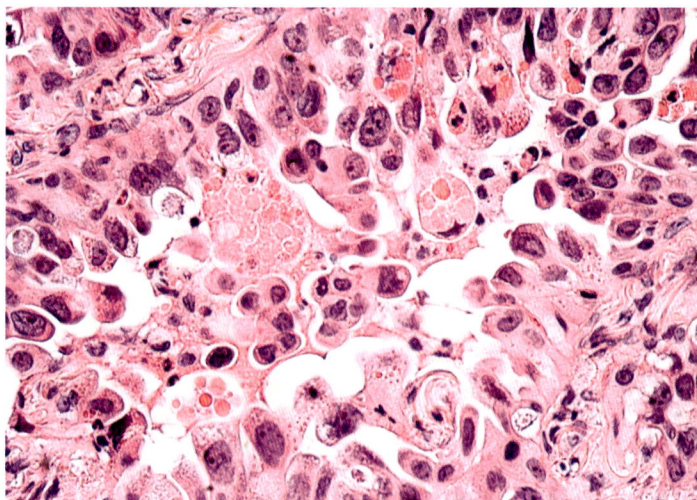

▲ *This photomicrograph image shows cancerous cells in the tissues of the lung.*

Contagious diseases are caused by germs such as bacteria and viruses. They include the common cold, flu and measles. Their spread can be controlled by good sanitation and hygiene, and also by vaccination.

Non-contagious diseases may be inherited or they may be caused by an injury, poor nutrition or hygiene, or ingesting harmful substances.

Autoimmune diseases are also non-contageous. These types of disorders are caused by body cells acting wrongly and attacking the body's own tissues.

Degenerative diseases occur in more elderly people as the body's tissues start to get older – and either do not function normally or gradually disappear.

Endemic diseases are diseases that occur in a particular area of the world, such as sleeping sickness in Africa.

DID YOU KNOW?
The most common disease in the world is tooth decay – so remember to brush your teeth!

The immune system

- The immune system is the complicated system of defences that your body uses to fight off attacks from germs and other invaders.

- Your body has a wide variety of barriers, toxic chemicals and traps that can prevent germs from entering it. The skin acts as a barrier that can stop many germs, as long as it is not broken.

- Mucus lines your airways and lungs to protect them from smoke particles – as well as invading germs. Your airways may fill with mucus when you have a cold, to limit the invasion of airborne germs.

- Itching, sneezing, coughing and vomiting are other ways in which the body can get rid of unwelcome invaders.

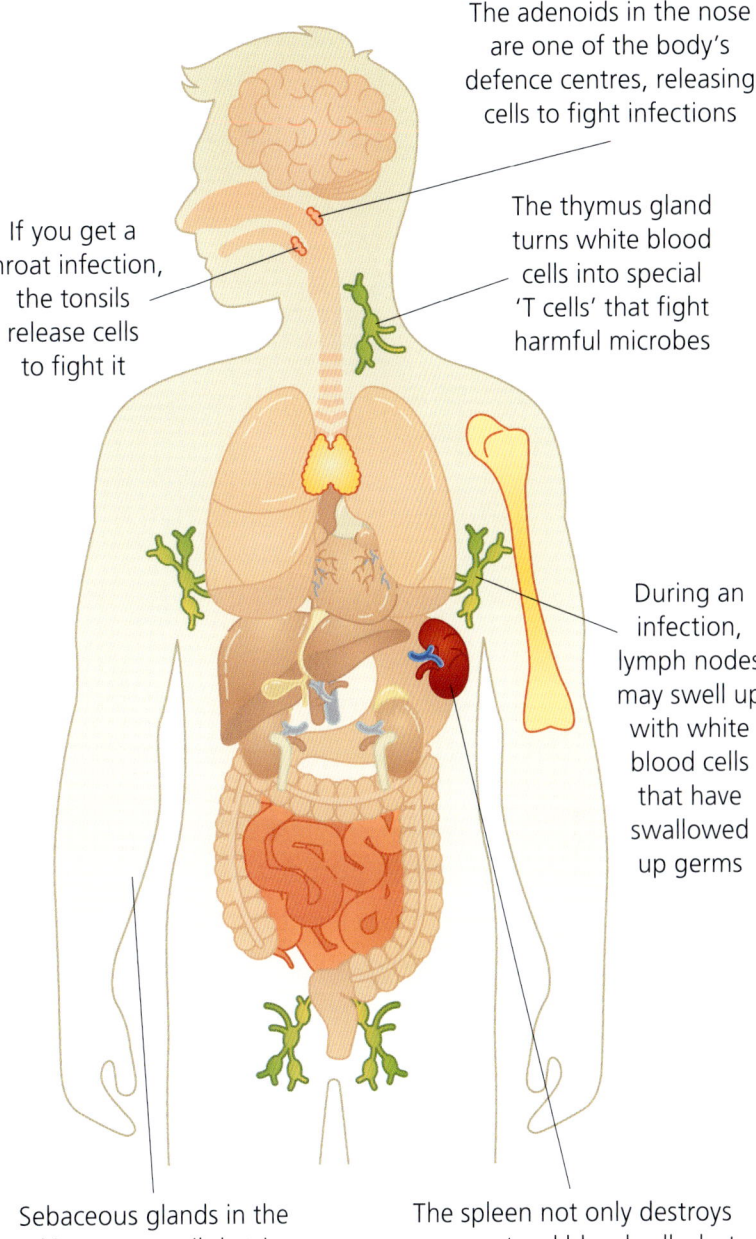

The adenoids in the nose are one of the body's defence centres, releasing cells to fight infections

If you get a throat infection, the tonsils release cells to fight it

The thymus gland turns white blood cells into special 'T cells' that fight harmful microbes

During an infection, lymph nodes may swell up with white blood cells that have swallowed up germs

Sebaceous glands in the skin ooze an oil that is poisonous to many bacteria

The spleen not only destroys worn-out red blood cells, but also helps to make antibodies and phagocytes

▲ The body's range of interior defences against infection is amazingly complex. The various types of white blood cells and the antibodies these defences make are particularly important.

The lymphatic system

The lymphatic system is your body's sewer, a network of pipes that drains waste from the cells.

It helps to protect the body against infection by filtering out infectious organisms and helps to keep the amount of fluid in the body stable.

The lymphatics are filled by a watery liquid called lymph fluid that, along with bacteria and waste chemicals, drains away from body tissues such as muscles.

The lymphatic system has no heart-like pump. Instead, lymphatic fluid is circulated (moved around) as a side effect of your heartbeat and muscle movement.

Lymph fluid drains back into the blood via the body's main vein, the superior vena cava.

The lymphatic system consists not only of the lymphatics and lymph nodes – but also includes the spleen, the thymus, the tonsils and the adenoids.

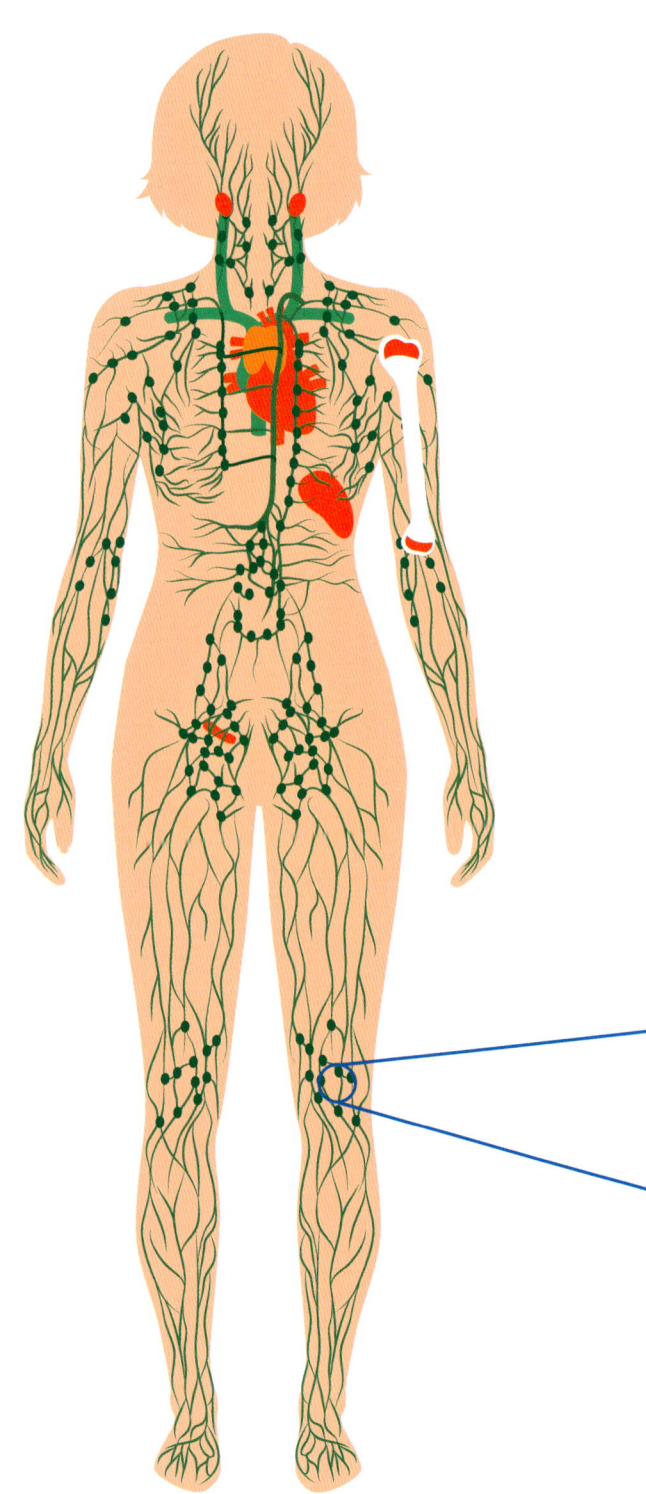

▲ *The lymphatic system is a branching network of little tubes that reaches throughout the body.*

Lymphocytes

- Lymphocytes are white blood cells that play a key role in the body's immune system, which targets invading germs.

- There are two main types of lymphocyte – B lymphocytes (B cells) and T lymphocytes (T cells).

- B cells develop into plasma cells that create antibodies for attacking bacteria – such as those that cause cholera – as well as some viruses.

- T cells work against viruses and other micro-organisms that hide inside body cells. They help to identify and destroy the invaded cells or their products. They also attack certain types of bacteria.

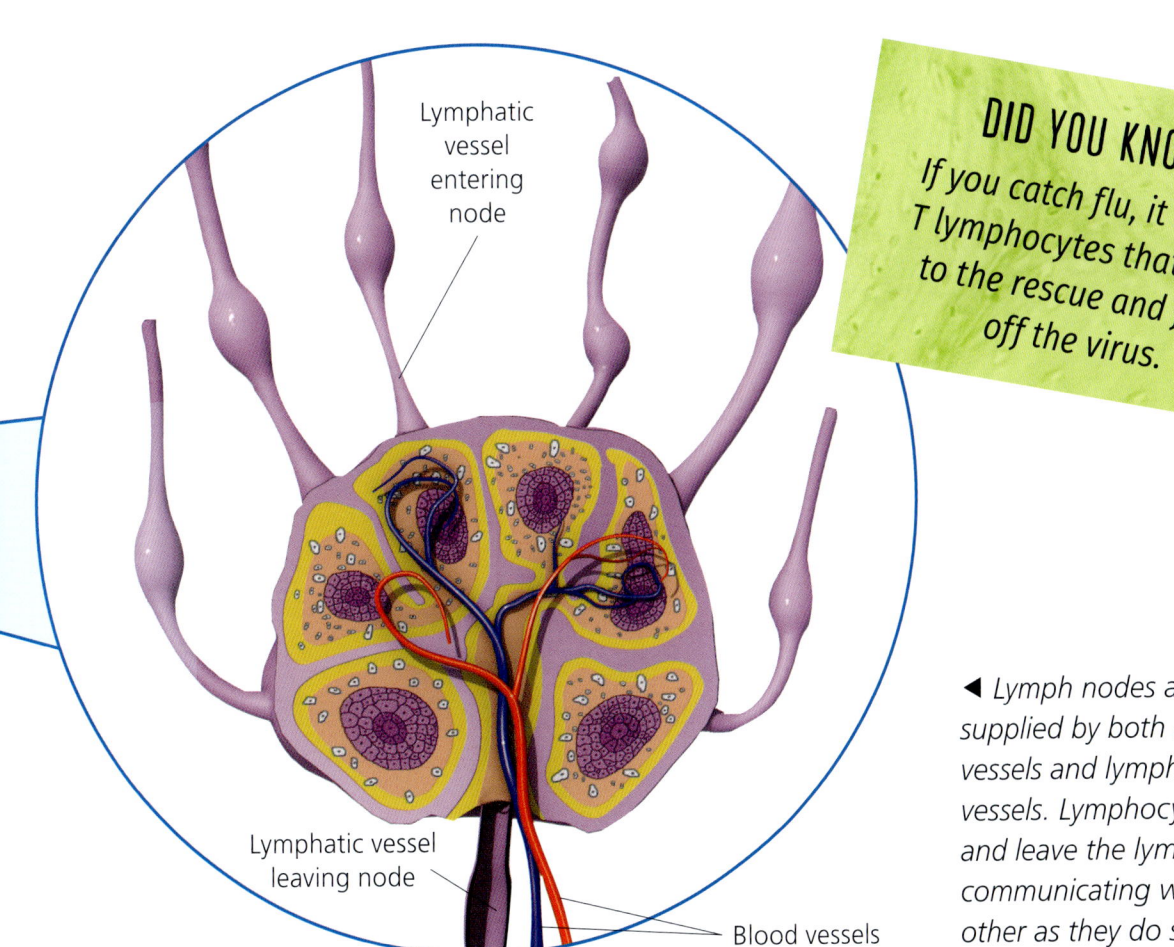

Lymphatic vessel entering node

Lymphatic vessel leaving node

Blood vessels

DID YOU KNOW?
If you catch flu, it is your T lymphocytes that come to the rescue and fight off the virus.

◀ *Lymph nodes are supplied by both blood vessels and lymphatic vessels. Lymphocytes enter and leave the lymph nodes, communicating with each other as they do so.*

137

Antibodies

Antibodies are tiny proteins that make germs vulnerable to attack from white blood cells called phagocytes.

Your body was armed from birth with antibodies for germs it had never even met. This is known as your innate immunity.

If your body comes across a germ it has no antibodies for, it quickly makes some. It then leaves 'memory' cells ready to be activated if the germ invades again. This is called acquired immunity.

DID YOU KNOW?
Human beings each generate around ten billion different antibodies.

Acquired immunity means you only suffer once from certain infections, such as chickenpox.

Allergies are sensitive reactions that occur in your body when too many antibodies are produced, or when they are created to attack antigens (foreign substances) that are actually harmless.

Autoimmune diseases are ones in which the body forms antibodies that act against its own tissue cells.

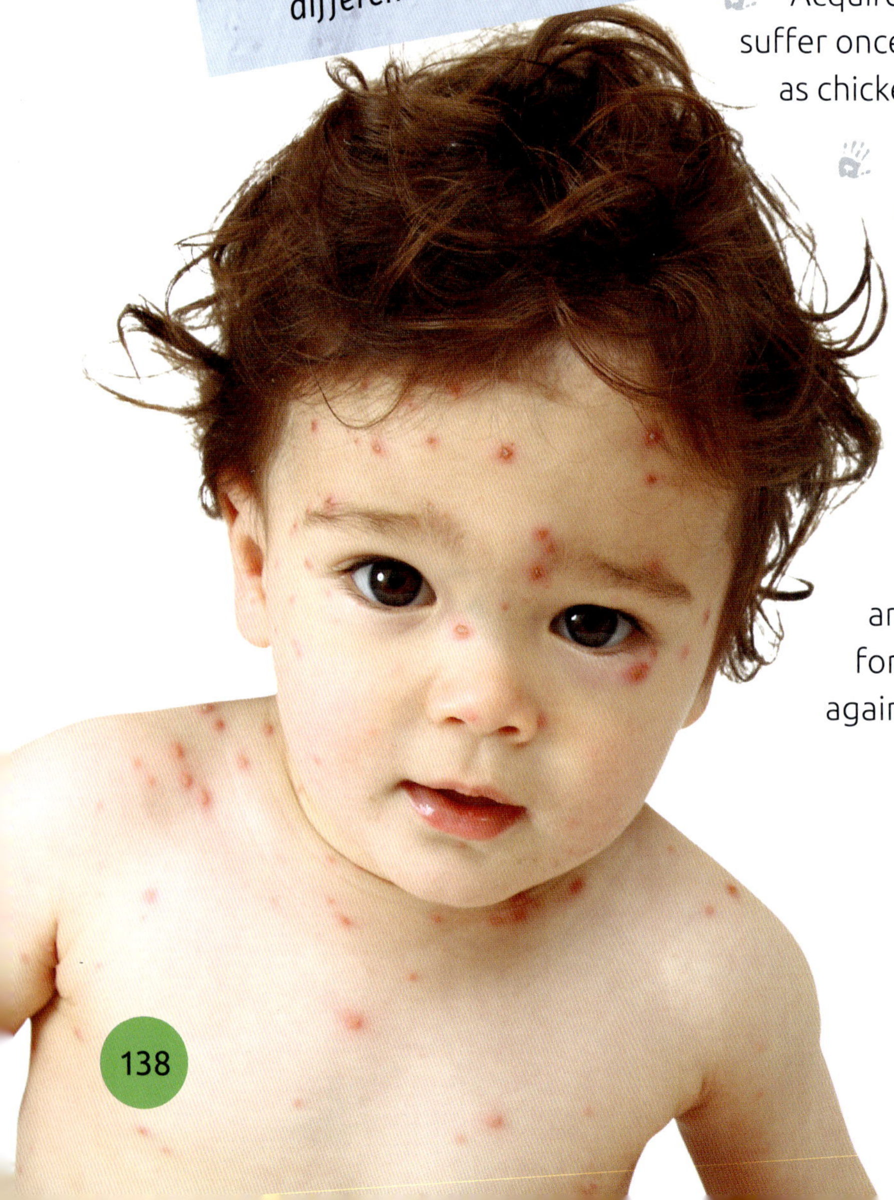

◄ *The body manufactures antibodies to the chickenpox virus, specially adapted for fighting off the illness.*

138

Vaccination

- Vaccination helps to protect you against an infectious disease by exposing you to a mild or dead version of the germ. This prompts your body to build up its own protection in the form of antibodies.

- Vaccination is also known as immunization, because it builds up your resistance or immunity to a disease.

- In passive immunization, you are injected with substances – such as antibodies – that have already been exposed to the germ. This gives you instant but short-lived protection.

▲ *Diseases such as diphtheria and whooping cough are now rare in many countries thanks to government vaccination programmes.*

- In active immunization, you are given a killed or otherwise harmless version of the germ. Your body then creates the antibodies itself, resulting in long-term protection.

- Children in many countries are given a series of vaccinations as they grow up, to protect them against diseases such as diphtheria, tetanus and polio.

- An updated flu vaccine is developed every year to protect against the current strain of the disease, which is always mutating (changing).

Index